MYTHS OF CHINA

WRITTEN BY XIAOBING WANG

DK

ILLUSTRATED BY KATIE PONDER

CONTENTS

JOURNEYS AND ADVENTURES

LOVE AND FRIENDSHIP

ABOUT THE MYTHS

A note for readers

As with all mythology, there are several different versions of Chinese myths, and our stories might contain some differences from the tales you have read elsewhere. While each storyteller brings a new perspective to the myths, the essential meanings behind the stories remain the same.

INTRODUCTION

Like many stories from ancient cultures, Chinese mythology reflects an understanding of nature and society. While many of these tales originate from ancient classics dating back thousands of years, evolving and growing through generations, others are more recent.

In much of Chinese mythology, there's an emphasis on unity and harmony between humans and the universe. Very often, gods and goddesses and heroes and heroines refuse to accept defeat and exude a spirit of self-reliance and independence.

The Chinese have created one of the most extensive and enduring civilizations in the world. I hope you enjoy this introduction to their exciting world and, as you travel back in time, catch a glimpse of life in a bygone age. Together, let us embark on this fascinating journey.

Xiaobing Wang

XIAOBING WANG, AUTHOR

LAND OF CHINA

The vast land of ancient China was at first quite isolated from the rest of the world. Its territory stretched across central and eastern Asia and was surrounded by deserts, mountains, and seas. China was sometimes a unified kingdom, and sometimes there were many divided small states. It then became united as a civilization.

LAKE BAIKAL is the "North Sea" of Chinese myth.

According to some sources, the Four Seas of Chinese myth are based on four real bodies of water that follow the north, south, east, and west boundaries of ancient China.

China is one of the world's oldest civilizations – it began about 5,000 years ago.

STATES AT WAR

From 475–221 BCE, ancient China was divided into several states which were often at war with each other. This time became known as the Warring States period. The competition and cooperation among these states led to a flourishing of Chinese philosophy.

FIRST EMPEROR

In 221 BCE, the king of the state of Qin conquered his rivals and became China's first Emperor: Qin Shi Huang. Qin (pronounced "Chin") gave its name to a new, unified China. The Great Wall was built largely under his reign. For the next two thousand years, China was to be an empire called the Middle Kingdom.

THE SILK ROAD

From around 130 BCE, a trading route called the Silk Road began to open the country up to outside influences. It stretched from China through central Asia and onto Europe. As well as goods being traded, ideas and religions were spread along the Silk Road.

BEGINNINGS

Like many ancient people, the Chinese turned to mythology to explain how the universe began and how we as humans came to be.

According to Chinese myth, the world began with chaos, unleashed when a being called Pangu cracked the egg he was in. This egg contained the two primal forces of Yin and Yang, which then separated to bring about order. And so, to the ancient Chinese, Yin and Yang were the fundamental driving forces behind the creation of all things.

Pangu and the Creation of the World

In the beginning, there was nothing but chaos in the form of an enormous egg. And the god Pangu was conceived within it.

After 18,000 years, Pangu awakened and found he was in a dark vastness. With a swing of his hands, he separated the chaos into two forces: Yin and Yang. These two forces were opposites, but were also interconnected.

And the heavy Yin sank, forming the earth, while the light Yang rose, creating the heavens.

Pangu stood between them and supported the sky to prevent them from reuniting. While the sky rose and the earth thickened, Pangu's body also grew.

After another 18,000 years, the structure of the heavens and earth took shape, and Pangu no longer worried about them rejoining.

Exhausted, he finally collapsed.

As Pangu neared death, his body underwent transformations that shaped the universe: his breath became the wind, his voice became thunder, his left eye became the sun, and his right eye became the moon.

His body turned into the mountains and the extremes of the world. His blood formed rivers and his muscles became fertile lands. His facial hair turned into the stars. His fur transformed into bushes and forests, and his bones became valuable minerals. Finally, his bone marrow became sacred diamonds deep beneath the earth, while in the sky above, his sweat fell as rain.

Pangu's left eye became the sun and his right eye became the moon.

How Nüwa Made Humankind

After Pangu created the heavens and the earth, the goddess Nüwa was dispatched to earth and lived on Mount Kunlun in northwestern China.

After a time Nüwa felt lonely, and she decided to create some companions for herself. She took some mud and water and began shaping little figures, calling them "people". These people were made in the image of the gods. They had a unique liveliness and natural charm that set them apart from other creatures. Surprisingly, they could even speak like Nüwa.

Excitedly, the newly created humans gathered around Nüwa, cheering and frolicking, before gradually dispersing across the land.

Nüwa desired to fill the world with more of her handcrafted beings to make the earth lively and vibrant. She tirelessly continued her work, shaping one after another. But the world was vast, and despite her efforts, humans remained scarce. Her hands became numb from the long hours of work.

Realizing that she needed a more efficient method to make humans, Nüwa looked around and found a nearby vine. She dipped it into a muddy pool and flung the mud onto the ground.

The tiny droplets of mud transformed into little humans, resembling those she had shaped with her hands.

This new method was faster, and Nüwa's excitement grew as she continued to sprinkle the mud across the earth. Soon, people were living in every part of the world, brought into existence by Nüwa's creative spirit. And from then on, the world was filled with the joyful presence of the humans she had made with her own hands.

How Nüwa Repaired the Sky

After they were created by Nüwa, humans multiplied and flourished, and lived happily for generations.

However, one year, the fire god Zhurong and the water god Gonggong became engaged in a fierce battle. Gonggong struck the supporting pillar of the heavens, Mount Buzhou, causing half of the sky to collapse. The impact created many holes in the sky. Water from the heavenly river poured down through the gaps and onto the earth, causing a terrible flood. Meteorites and fires fell from the torn sky, bringing devastation to the people below.

Seeing how people were suffering,
Nüwa decided to take action.

She gathered together special five-coloured stones and used them to mend the shattered sky. The Divine Turtle of the Eastern Sea sacrificed its feet to support the four corners of the world. But Nüwa realized that she did not have enough stones to complete the task.

Nüwa knew there was only one solution.

She used her own body to fill the last gaping hole in the sky. Nüwa had sacrificed her life so that tranquillity could be restored between the heavens and the earth. The skies were adorned with colourful clouds and rainbows, and all creatures once again thrived on the renewed and harmonious earth.

FUXI

CREATOR GOD

The god Fuxi is said to have taught people to understand the laws of nature and society. He invented the Eight Trigrams – a set of symbols that represents the eight basic principles of reality. Fuxi also established the institution of marriage, and promoted Chinese culture and music.

SACRED SYMBOLS

EIGHT TRIGRAMS
The Eight Trigrams, or Bagua, has its roots in Taoist beliefs. Each of the eight trigrams is made up of three whole or broken lines that represent either Yin (broken line) or Yang (continuous line).

GREAT INVENTOR

Fuxi invented many things, including writing, and nets for fishing, and he even thought up the marriage system. He also invented musical instruments like the zither, and composed melodies and songs.

GODDESS

NÜWA

MOTHER OF HUMANITY

The goddess Nüwa is the twin sister of Fuxi and is considered one of the divine beings involved in the creation of heaven and earth. Nüwa is the mother of humanity, protecting all people and ensuring the continuity and inheritance of future generations.

SACRED SYMBOLS

FIVE-COLOURED CRYSTALS
To mend the sky, Nüwa used magical crystals, each one made up of five colours – blue, yellow, red, white, and black.

MUD AND WATER
It is said that the goddess Nüwa created all people from two basic elements: mud and water.

EARTH
In some accounts, Nüwa went as far as sacrificing her own body to mend earth's sky.

MOUNT KUNLUN
This mythical mountain is said to be in northwest China. Here, Nüwa made her home.

SAVING HUMANITY

The most destructive wars arose from humanity itself. Nüwa was the mother of humankind, and she was also the inventive goddess who saved the world from human catastrophe.

Fuxi and the Eight Trigrams

In ancient times, there was a young woman named Huaxu who visited a place called Leize for a holiday.

While exploring, she came across a gigantic footprint and, with great curiosity, stepped on it. To her great surprise, she became pregnant. Huaxu carried the child for twelve years before giving birth to a son whom she named Fuxi. The boy was no ordinary human being, and grew up to be part human, part python.

Fuxi united various tribes and established his capital in the Chen region.

He observed the clouds in the sky, the rain and snow falling, the thunder and lightning, the strong winds and thick fogs on the ground, as well as the movement of birds and animals. Inspired by what he saw, he created the Eight Trigrams, which were made up of eight simple yet profound symbols that summarized all things between heaven and earth.

Imitating the spiders' webs in nature, Fuxi created nets for fishing and hunting. Observing animal behaviours, he taught people how to domesticate wild animals. Fuxi was keen for couples to live together in peace and harmony, and he established the marriage system. He also invented writing, which replaced the old method of recording information of tying knots in ropes.

Fuxi's creativity extended to music and instruments.

He invented musical instruments like the zither, composed songs, and introduced music into people's lives.

It is said that Fuxi's contributions enriched the culture of ancient China, leaving an enduring legacy that continues to shape Chinese traditions and beliefs.

The Father of Farming and Medicine

Shennong, born with the head of an ox and the body of a human, became the leader of the Yan tribe, in the scorching south of China.

The Yan people survived by foraging for wild fruits and eating raw shellfish. Sadly, many suffered from poisoning and their lives were often cut short. To help his people live longer and stay healthy, Shennong embarked on a long journey of exploration.

Scaling mountains and crossing valleys, Shennong tirelessly tasted countless plants and herbs.

He searched for remedies to treat illnesses and to cleanse the body. He discovered that rice, wheat, millet, barley, and beans could provide nourishment.

Shennong found various medicinal herbs that could fight poisons and maintain good health. He experimented with herbs and keenly observed how plants changed with the seasons and favoured different types of soil.

Shennong used this knowledge to guide people in agricultural practices, allowing them to plan fruit collection and seed planting in an organized way.

This is how Shennong created the foundation for Chinese agriculture.

Shennong delved into the preparation of medicines, studying their relationship with specific illnesses. Through countless experiments, he gained a wealth of medicinal knowledge, which was recorded and passed down.

And so, for many years to come, Shennong was known and revered as the Divine Farmer and God of Medicine.

The Discovery of Fire

Long ago, early humans relied on simple stone tools to hunt for food. People ate raw meat or plant roots and leaves. They wore animal skins or clothing made from woven plant materials.

They used stone blocks and other tools as weapons to defend themselves against wild animals. Because of their raw diet, they were prone to diseases and injuries, and so their lives were often short. At this time, forest fires were common, caused by the dry conditions and the hot, beating sun. People viewed fire as dangerous and did not understand that it could also be very useful.

Then, in the region of Shangqiu, a wise man emerged. While others avoided fire, he would approach it wherever it was present.

The man sought out places where there was fire. Through careful observation, he discovered that fire had many benefits.

When other people stumbled upon small animals burnt by fire, they would discard them. But the man noticed that the burnt animals had become pieces of meat that could be eaten. Consuming cooked rather than raw meat reduced the unpleasant smell and felt better on the stomach. So he encouraged the people around him to roast the animals they captured over a fire, slowly breaking their habit of eating raw animal flesh.

During cold weather, the wise man noticed that being in sunlight or near a fire provided comfort to the body. The man showed people how to gather round a fire when it was cold.

And so the wise man grasped the knowledge of fire and understood how it could be useful.

To ensure that fire was readily available for all, the wise man worked out how people could make fire for themselves. After lots of experimenting, he eventually discovered two methods – the friction method of drilling wood and the percussion method of striking stones. Since flint was used in the making of fire, and the Chinese word for flint is "sui", people came to know him as Suirenshi – the God of Fire.

GOD

SHENNONG

GOD OF FARMING AND MEDICINE

Shennong, also known as the Divine Farmer, is seen as the ancestor of Chinese agriculture and medicine. He developed techniques for growing crops, studied medicinal herbs, and helped to improve medical treatment.

SACRED SYMBOLS

CROPS
According to legend, Shennong taught people how to sow crops, such as rice and wheat.

PLOUGH
It is said that Shennong invented the plough and taught early farmers how to use it.

HERBS
Shennong experimented with different herbs so that people knew what to avoid or use.

MEDICAL BOOK
Shennong's insights on medicinal herbs were compiled in the book *Shennong Ben Cao Jing*.

MEDICAL TESTER

Shennong was not afraid to take risks with his own health in the search for medical knowledge. He is said to have suffered poisoning seventy times a day while tasting different species of plants.

SUIRENSHI

GOD OF FIRE

Suirenshi is regarded as the creator of fire. Legend has it that Suirenshi taught people to use wood and stone to create fire, bringing its benefits to humanity and improving their way of life. It is said that an owl-like bird helped him to discover fire.

SACRED SYMBOLS

BIRTHPLACE
Suirenshi is said to have been born in the ancient Chinese city of Shangqiu.

SUI TREE
Suirenshi first saw fire shooting from the Sui tree. The tree had a wide canopy of leaves and long roots.

WOOD AND STONE
Suirenshi helped people to make fire with stones as well as dry wood.

FIRE
Suirenshi is a good and benevolent fire god. The other fire god, Zhurong, is much more destructive.

HOW SUIRENSHI OBSERVED FIRE

The story goes that Suirenshi saw an owl-like bird pecking at the fire-bearing wood of the Sui tree. The bird continued pecking until fire shot out. Suirenshi then took a small branch to drill for fire.

How Leizu Discovered Silk

A long time ago, in a distant land called Xiling, there lived a young ruler called Leizu, who had great artistic sense.

Her people draped themselves in clothing made from leaves, tree bark, and animal hides. These garments provided warmth, but lacked the elegance and beauty Leizu longed for.

Leizu noticed the webs that spiders weave were made of a material that was lightweight and breathable. However, the silk was fragile and would easily break.

Driven by her quest for finer and stronger materials, Leizu set off on a journey through the wilderness.

After many trials, she stumbled upon the silken coverings, called cocoons, that some insects made. These cocoons were strong, and impossible to unravel. So Leizu sat down to think. She rested beneath a mulberry tree and brewed a cup of tea. Then, on looking down, Leizu saw that a silkworm cocoon had fallen into her tea cup.

Gently lifting the cocoon with a stick, Leizu discovered that the boiling tea had loosened its fine silk fibres. She twisted several strands together, creating

strong threads, and then weaved the threads into a fabric: silk.

Within a few days, delicate moths had emerged, each laying hundreds of eggs. The following year, the hatchlings were fed mulberry leaves and grew into healthy silkworms.

With time, these silkworms spun larger and finer cocoons.

Meanwhile, the legendary Yellow Emperor was emerging as a powerful force and his tribe was rapidly expanding. When Leizu's people crossed paths with the Yellow Emperor's tribe, they discovered a stark difference in their way of life. Leizu's tribe favoured the simple life – one where they were content to live off the land and focus on spiritual well-being. In contrast, the Yellow Emperor's people were keen to make progress in technology and were more ambitious. However, the two styles complemented each other, and they found they could live in harmony. Leizu fell in love with the Yellow Emperor and married him, and their marriage strengthened the tie between the two tribes.

Leizu shared her knowledge of silk craftsmanship with other people, teaching them to cultivate mulberry trees and raise silkworms. The art of silk farming began to flourish all over China, bringing prosperity to its people.

The Three Sage Kings

Some years after the Yellow Emperor ruled, there were three Sage Kings – Yao, Shun, and Yü.

The first Sage King, Yao, had had a miraculous birth. His mother had been walking by a river when she was visited by a Red Dragon. Fourteen months later she gave birth to a baby boy, whom they named Yao. From a young age Yao showed great ability, and became ruler at only eighteen years of age. He proved to be a good man and a capable king.

Yao had a son called Dan Zhu, who was particularly fond of playing the game of Go.

This game of strategy was played on a board – it was complicated and very absorbing, so much so that Dan Zhu was more interested in playing Go than learning from his father about how to govern the country.

Yao watched with sadness this failing in his son. He realized that Dan Zhu would not make a great ruler. With great wisdom he knew he should put the good of the country before his own family. And so Yao sought to find someone who was worthy of the position.

A man called Shun came to Yao's attention. Shun had lost his mother at a young age, and his father, the Blind Old Man, had remarried. This Old Man loved his second wife, and they had a child together – another boy. Tragically, the couple lost interest in Shun and were cruel to him.

Despite his unhappy upbringing, Shun treated his father and new family with love and respect. Yao observed this noble behaviour, and knew that Shun would make a worthy successor.

Shun understood that the power of a king came with great responsibility, and he ruled virtuously.

However, Shun in turn found that his own son, Shang Jun, was more interested in having a good time singing and dancing than in becoming a great leader. So, rather than asking his son, Shun appointed a man called Yü to take over an important flood-control project. Yü's success in managing this task earned him the love of the people and the backing of influential ministers. Eventually, Yü ascended to the throne.

Upon becoming king, Yü, having learned from the experiences of Yao and Shun, carefully trained his son, Qi, to become a leader. Eventually, Qi succeeded his father to the throne, marking the beginning of the first Chinese dynasty in which emperors or kings passed on power to the next generation.

The Calming of the Flood

In ancient times, the central plains were once plagued by devastating floods that submerged crops and houses, forcing many people to leave their homes.

A man called Gùn was appointed to tackle the problem. He led a team that installed barriers to try to block the floods. However, despite nine years of effort, the floods remained. Eventually, Gùn lost his job and tragically passed away.

The people then chose Gùn's son, Yu, to undertake the challenge.

At that time, Yu had just got married. Tearfully bidding farewell to his beloved wife, he set off with a group of assistants and travelled tirelessly to the central plains. With a plumb line in his left hand and a measuring rod in his right, Yu meticulously studied the flow of rivers and

the direction of the mountains. Learning from his father's experience of using blockades, Yu developed a new method to control water. His plan was to build several channels that would allow the water to flow smoothly into the sea. Yu laboured hard, eating and sleeping on the construction site. And then news came to him that his wife had given birth to a son.

Yu longed to return home to see his wife and child, but the huge task of quelling the floods compelled him to stay.

With tears in his eyes, Yu continued to work. He levelled the land where needed and then finally created the channels. After thirteen years of effort, Yu and his workers tamed the roaring rivers into gentle streams that flowed eastward.

From that day on, large areas of land became fertile, allowing people to live prosperous and contented lives.

His work completed, Yu mounted his horse and travelled home to be reunited with his beloved wife and to meet his son for the first time.

Yi and the Ten Suns

In the vast East Sea stood a divine tree called Fusang, on which perched ten three-legged crows. They were the sons of the Eastern God Emperor, Jun, and the radiant light they emitted became the sun that people saw.

Each sun – perched on a two-wheeled chariot – took it in turns to traverse the heavens, spreading light and warmth to every corner of the world. The ten suns rotated daily, maintaining harmony between heaven and earth.

People lived contently. They were grateful for the sun, which brought them time, brightness, and happiness. They often looked up at the sky in worship.

However, as time went on, the ten suns grew arrogant and yearned to travel the sky together. So one day, at dawn, they all climbed onto the chariot at the same time.

The sky was then filled with ten scorching suns. The intense heat set forests on fire. Crops and orchards became withered and burnt, leaving people and livestock without food. Many people either perished in the scorching heat or became weak and were easy prey for wild beasts. Those who survived the inferno desperately searched for shelter and life-saving water and food, while ferocious animals and poisonous insects took advantage of the chaos to prey on the weakened humans.

News reached the heavens, and Emperor Jun was furious. He summoned a young and handsome hero named Yi, who was a skilled archer. Yi was given a red bow and a bag of white arrows, and instructed to descend to the mortal world. His mission was to discipline the ten unruly suns.

Yi journeyed across ninety-nine tall mountains and through ninety-nine deserts to reach the shore of the East Sea.

Yi climbed a great mountain, and at its foot lay the boundless sea. He looked up at the sky. The ten suns paid no attention to Yi and continued their arrogant display in the sky. Yi was furious and drew his bow.

One by one, Yi shot arrows at nine of the suns. And as he did so he pierced nine of the ten three-legged crows...

The crows fell dead, one after another. Their feathers scattered on the ground, and their light and heat vanished.

The people instantly felt a refreshing coolness and rejoiced.

The cheers echoed to the heavens. However, Emperor Jun, seeing that nine of his sons had died, erupted in anger, forbidding Yi from returning to the heavenly court. He also commanded the surviving sun to roam the sky day after day without rest. And so from then on, this sun rose from the Eastern Sea every day and set on the western mountains at night. This sun provided warmth to the mortal realm and sustained all living beings, enabling people to live in peace and prosperity.

Yi drew his bow and shot down nine of the ten suns.

JADE EMPEROR

GOD

THE EMPEROR OF HEAVEN

Originally a mortal, the Jade Emperor was kind, wise, and helped the needy. Because of his many good deeds, he was finally made immortal. Many years later, he was chosen by a panel of sages to become the ruler of all things.

SACRED SYMBOLS

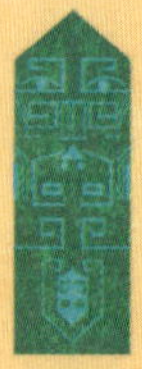

JADE
The green gemstone jade is highly prized in China. It is a symbol of purity and spirituality.

TAOISM
The Jade Emperor is seen by Taoists as the ruler of heaven, earth, and the underworld.

CHINESE BUDDHISM
The Jade Emperor is a spiritual figure, who has often been linked with Chinese Buddhism.

HEAVENLY LIGHT
When he was born, it is said that the Jade Emperor gave out a heavenly light.

KITCHEN HELPER
The Jade Emperor had many gods gathered around to help him. One of the most important was Zao Jun, known as the Kitchen God because people kept a picture of him in their kitchens.

GODDESS

XIWANGMU

QUEEN MOTHER OF THE WEST

Sitting by the side of the Jade Emperor in the heavenly court is Xiwangmu, or the Queen Mother of the West. Xiwangmu was once a wild demon. However, after repenting of her evil ways, she achieved enlightenment and became a goddess.

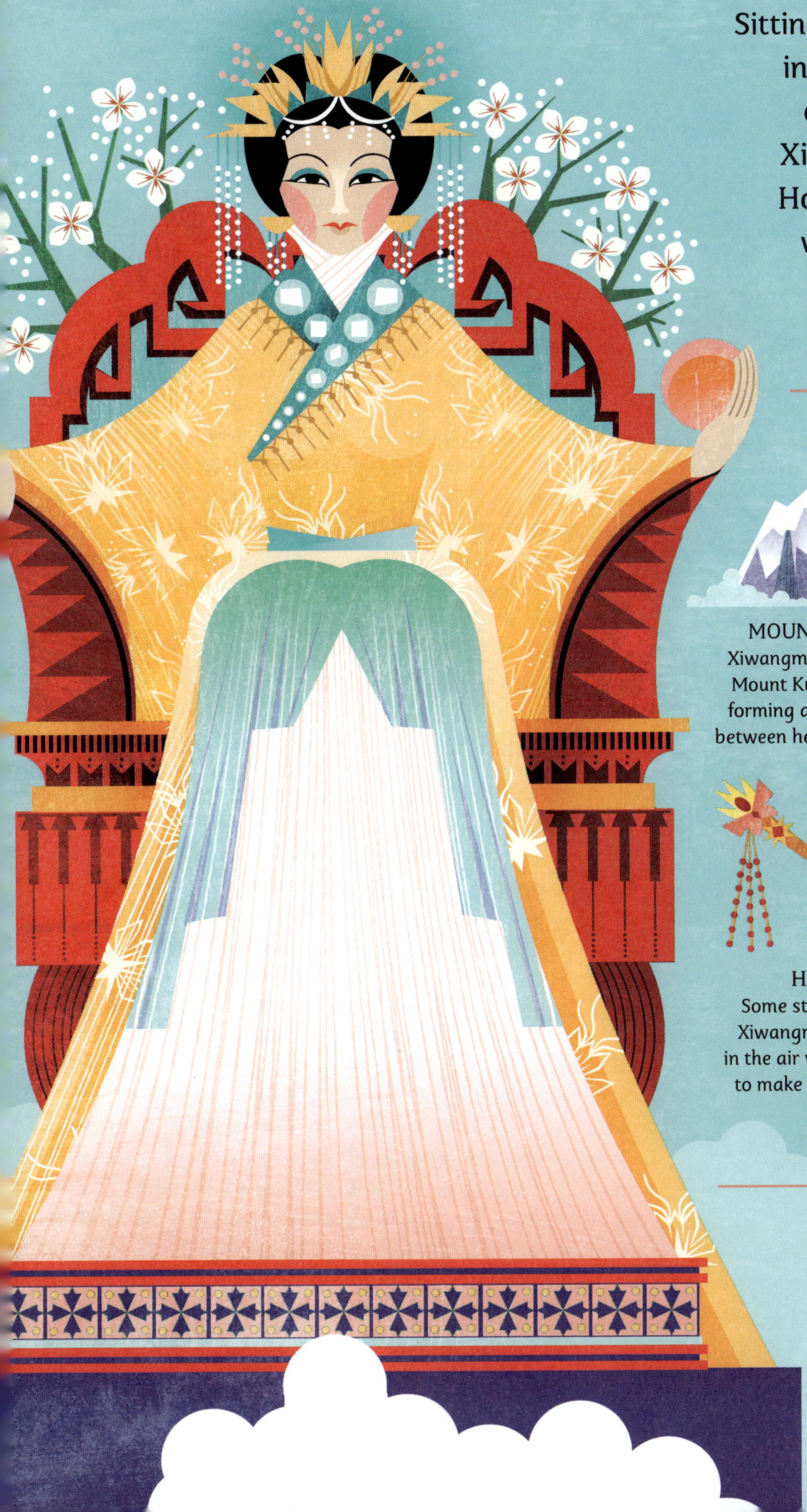

SACRED SYMBOLS

MOUNT KUNLUN
Xiwangmu's palace is on Mount Kunlun – a peak forming a meeting place between heaven and earth.

PEACHES
In her palace garden, Xiwangmu serves peaches to her guests, making them immortal.

HAIRPIN
Some stories say that Xiwangmu drew a line in the air with her hairpin to make the Milky Way.

THE BIG DIPPER
Xiwangmu is the controller of time and space, and one of her symbols is the Big Dipper constellation.

TIGER-GODDESS
As a demon goddess, Xiwangmu has the teeth of a tiger and a leopard's tail. She wears a jade crown on top of her wild hair.

Chang'e Ascends to the Moon

It came to pass that Yi the heavenly archer met a beautiful woman called Chang'e. He fell in love with her, and she with him, and they got married.

Yi was a hero renowned for rescuing the people on earth, and many became his followers. They sought to learn martial arts from him, including a cunning and greedy man called Pang Meng.

At the same time, the goddess Xiwangmu had long admired Yi's skilfulness and she gave him an elixir that granted him the ability to ascend to heaven and become an immortal. However, Yi was unwilling to part with his wife, Chang'e, and he entrusted the elixir to her for safekeeping in a treasure box.

Now, it so happened that the greedy, untrustworthy Pang Meng found out about the elixir and was desperate to get his hands on it.

One morning, when Yi was away, Pang Meng stole into the couple's home and tried to persuade Chang'e to hand over the elixir. But Chang'e knew that this man spelt trouble. She refused to surrender the elixir and in the end had to make a tough decision. To avoid the elixir of immortaility falling into the hands of Pang Meng, she swallowed the potion herself.

Upon taking the elixir, Chang'e floated up to heaven. As she did not want to stay too far from her husband and the people, she landed on the moon that is the nearest to earth, becoming a goddess of the moon.

Yi returned home, only to find that his beloved wife was missing.

Frantically searching for her, he looked up to the sky and saw the moon casting its silvery glow, with a shadowy image of his wife standing near a cinnamon tree.

Yi called out to her, desperately trying to reach her, but she remained unattainable in the heavens.

The villagers dearly missed the good and kind-hearted Chang'e and prepared her favourite foods in the courtyard, sending their blessings to her.

From then on, every year on the fifteenth day of the eighth lunar month, people celebrate the Mid-Autumn Festival, hoping for a reunion with their loved ones, just as Yi longed for his wife's return.

Yi looked up at the moon and saw his beloved wife, Chang'e.

Chang'e and the Jade Rabbit

Once Chang'e had ascended to the moon, she found herself consumed by an unending longing for her beloved Yi.

Having consumed the elixir that granted her immortality and eternal youth, Chang'e watched helplessly as Yi grew older. She remembered how Yi had not taken the elixir, as he had wanted to age alongside Chang'e. Now, she found herself immortal but separated from her beloved, forced to witness him become older while she remained eternally youthful.

Chang'e sought help from the Queen Mother of the West, hoping to reunite with her love, even if it meant surrendering her own immortality.

She was willing to return to earth and age alongside Yi, cherishing their twilight years together.

However, the Queen Mother of the West could not easily undo the effects of the elixir. The most she could offer Chang'e was a bittersweet choice: Yi could become immortal and join her on the moon, but he would have to take on a different form – that of a rabbit. He would also have to forget his past life and memories, erasing all recollection of their love. No matter how much Chang'e wanted to, she would not be able to reveal their past to him, as it would result in his immediate death.

Chang'e was heartbroken but realized that this was the only way to save Yi from eternal suffering. And so she agreed.

As he sipped the soup of oblivion, Yi transformed into a small white rabbit. His memories of Chang'e and their love faded away, replaced by the simple mind of a rabbit, as he slowly ascended to the moon.

Chang'e caressed her transformed beloved, and called him Jade Rabbit.

She longed to share their past and the depth of their love with him, but her promise kept her silent.

Chang'e was determined to find some comfort, however. She immersed herself in the mystical arts, researching ways to restore Yi's human form and memories. Finally, she gave the Jade Rabbit the job of mixing the elixir of life.

Their days on the moon turned into years, and their bond deepened. The moon, with its serene beauty and enigmatic charm, became their haven, a place where love transcends time and memory.

On a clear night, when you look up and gaze at the moon, you may see Chang'e reading a book and the Jade Rabbit holding a pestle to pound a mixture that is the elixir of life.

MAGICAL CREATURES

Mythical stories from China are full of enigmatic and extraordinary beings – from helpful and wise creatures to frightening-looking monsters who scare whole neighbourhoods.

Some are shape-shifters, changing into human form, while others are symbols, such as the animals that represent the years in the Chinese calendar. Many of these beings inspire curiosity about the unknown, and none more so than the Great Peng, flying high above in the heavens, beating its wings for evermore.

The Great Peng

In the Northern Ocean, there was a fish called Kun, a creature of immense size that stretched across a vast distance.

The fish swam gracefully through the wide blue sea and moved with ease in the deep currents. Content with its existence, Kun believed it could conquer the turbulent waves and dominate the sea.

After hundreds of years, Kun had explored all the Northern Ocean. And so, it set its sights on the distant Southland, an untamed and pure land with infinite potential, which remained unexplored. It saw that the vastness of the sky surpassed the vastness of the sea, and that the limitless heights beckoned. So, although a fish, Kun yearned to venture beyond the sea and explore boundless skies.

One day, Kun underwent a miraculous metamorphosis. The fish transformed into a majestic bird called the Great Peng.

Peng had feathers that seemed to span thousands of miles when fully extended. The bird soared freely through the heavens, stretching its wings. With its majestic neck, the Great Peng flew over the rivers

and seas, believing it could surpass even the gods themselves.

One day, as Peng was flying south to the Lake of Heaven, the quail, living in a small puddle, ridiculed it, asking the bird where it was going.

"When I fly, I only rise a short distance and then come back down. I fly freely between the wild hemp, and I am quite happy and content. So, where do you want to fly to?"

Nearby, the cicada echoed these thoughts, "Whenever I want to fly, I just take off for a bit and land on an elm tree. Sometimes, if I don't have enough strength to fly high, I jump from one hedgerow into another. Why bother flying nine thousand miles high, going all the way to that distant South Sea?"

As if nothing had been said, the Great Peng continued to circle the heavenly skies. Alas! How could ordinary creatures understand the extraordinary being that is the Great Peng?

And so, with the beating of the birds' wings, the universe continues for evermore.

The Chinese Phoenix and the Hundred Birds

Long ago, there was a great flock of birds that included one special bird called the Chinese Phoenix. It was slightly bigger than the other birds, and had very few feathers.

One warm summer, the Chinese Phoenix, who also went by the name of Fenghuang, thought to itself, "Finding food is easy now, but in winter, it won't be so simple. I should start storing some food in advance." When the other birds heard this idea, they mocked Fenghuang. "Even if winter comes, we're not afraid," they said. "We don't believe there won't be any food left, and besides, it's still a long time away. Why rush?"

However, the Chinese Phoenix did not give up on its idea. The bird kept busy flying to different places, collecting various fruits, and bringing them back to its nest. Every winter, no matter how harsh it was, Fenghuang always had enough to eat. And this kindly creature would willingly share its food with any hungry little birds it encountered.

One year, winter arrived early, and the birds of the forest couldn't find any food.

In the freezing cold, birds became so hungry and weak they fell to the ground. Seeing this, the Chinese Phoenix became very worried.

It gathered all the birds and said, "I have stored plenty of food here. Let's save and eat together. It should be enough to get us through this difficult time." The birds were very grateful for Fenghuang's generous help and they managed to survive the harsh winter.

Spring arrived, and the weather gradually warmed up.

All the birds wanted to show their gratitude to Fenghuang. They plucked their most beautiful feathers and crafted a dazzling garment, which they presented to the Chinese Phoenix, electing the creature as the Bird King.

From then on, every year on Fenghuang's birthday, birds from all around would fly to congratulate it. And this celebration became known as the "Chinese Phoenix and the Hundred Birds".

The Legend of the White Snake

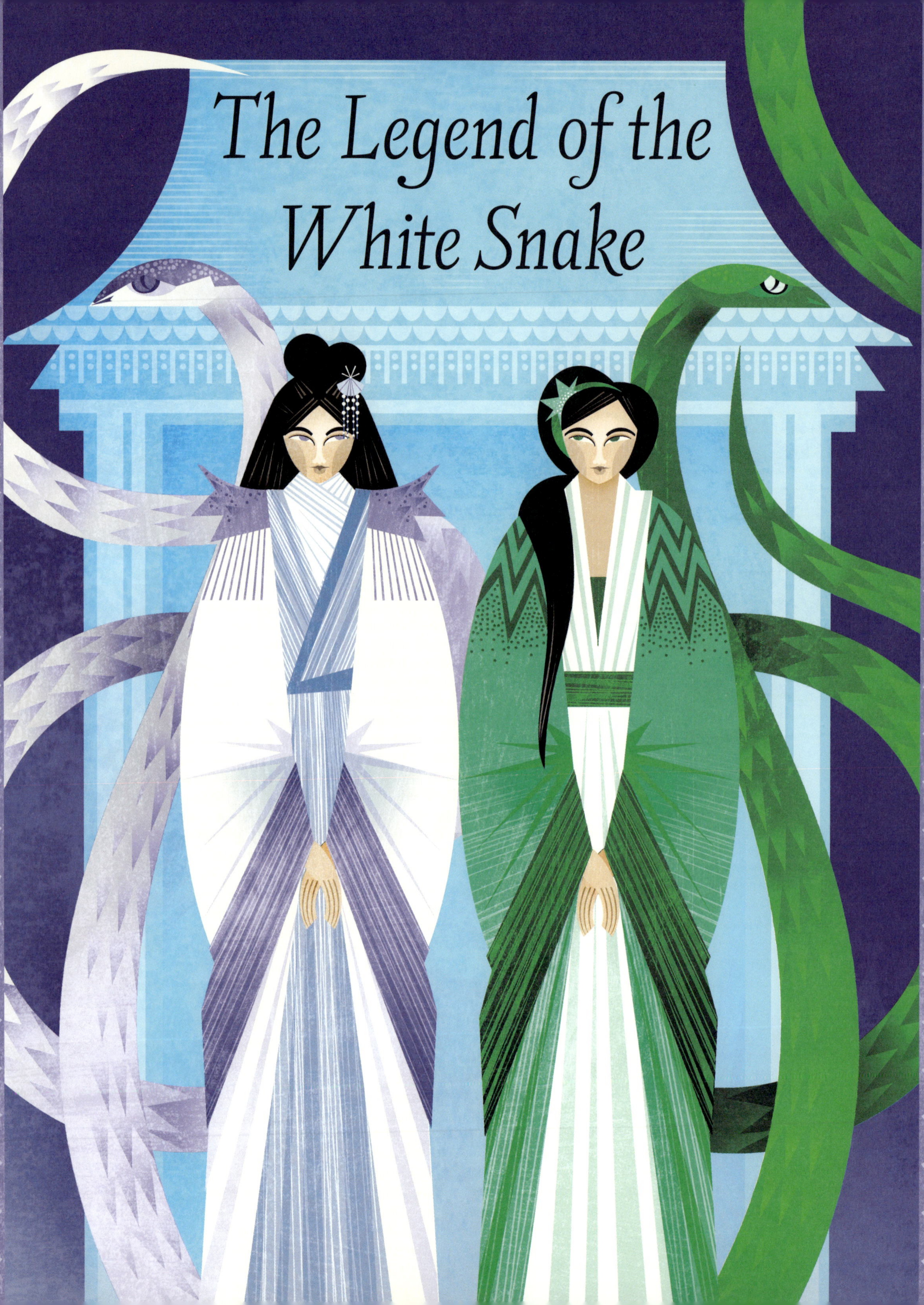

Once, there was a Zen Buddhist monk who died having reached full spiritual enlightenment, called nirvana. A student called Lü Bo wished to organize a ceremony in his teacher's honour.

So Lü Bo put some relics of the monk in a sachet, and then burned incense to offer respect. On his way back from the ceremony, Lü Bo met someone about to kill a white snake. Not wanting to see the snake harmed, he bought the creature and set it free.

Wishing to repay him, the white snake followed Lü Bo to his house. However, the snake accidentally ate some relics that belonged to the monk. From this, the snake gained a thousand years of spiritual development. Years passed, and Lü Bo eventually died at a great old age.

The white snake transformed into a beautiful woman and appeared near the Yingbo Bridge on the Su Causeway.

There, she saw a beggar holding a green snake, planning to take out its gallbladder for money. The white snake-woman realized that the green snake was also a spiritual being, and so she bought it. They became sworn sisters.

It came to pass that Lü Bo was reincarnated, and he became a man called Xu Xian. The white snake wanted to thank him. So, the two snakes, both in female form, travelled to the city of Hangzhou. Here, the white snake-woman asked to borrow an umbrella from Xu Xian. The two became better acquainted and they fell in love.

The couple soon got married and moved to Zhenjiang, where they ran a medicine shop.

Meanwhile, the Zen monk had also been reincarnated. He was now a monk called Fahai, who continued his spiritual development at the Jinshan Temple in Zhenjiang. When Fahai encountered his former disciple, Xu Xian, he noticed demonic energy surrounding him. He did not understand why this was so at first, but then learned that both the white and green snakes were demons. Since Fahai's duty was to subdue demonic life, he tried to explain to Xu Xian the snake-woman's true nature.

At first, Xu Xian would not believe Fahai. After all, he loved his wife very much.

However, Fahai persuaded Xu Xian to use cinnabar wine to intoxicate his wife, and so reveal her true form. Upon seeing his beloved wife momentarily turn into a white snake,

Xu Xian collapsed in fear. Then the white snake-woman, holding back her sadness, risked her life to seek immortal herbs on Mount Emei to revive Xu Xian.

After Xu Xian had recovered, the white snake-woman admitted her true identity but told him that her love was true and that nothing could stand between them. Xu Xian regretted not trusting her, and knew he still loved her.

Through the love they shared, the white snake-woman soon became pregnant.

Fahai, however, did not want to give up. He imprisoned Xu Xian in the Jinshan Temple and forced him to become a monk. To rescue Xu Xian, the white snake-woman, with the help of the green snake-woman, finally confronted Fahai.

In an effort to rescue Xu Xian, the two women brought forth water from the West Lake and flooded the Jinshan Temple, where Xu Xian was imprisoned. Although they did not mean to do this, the flood affected a large area and killed many innocent people. Due to her pregnancy, however, the white snake-woman's power was limited, and she was not able to defeat Fahai.

In the chaos, Xu Xian took the opportunity to escape back to Hangzhou and was reunited with his wife near the Broken Bridge over the West Lake. There, she gave birth to their child – a boy – naming him Xu Shilin.

Taking advantage of the snake-woman's weakness after childbirth, Fahai imprisoned her in a Buddhist bowl and kept her under the Leifeng Pagoda.

In despair, the snake-woman pleaded with Fahai to release her, saying, "I have a child, and I have to be there to care for him." Fahai pointed at the sago palm tree in front of the pagoda and said, "When this sago palm tree blossoms, you will be free." However, this tree had not bloomed in five hundred years.

For the next twenty years, the green snake-woman and Xu Xian took care of the child Xu Shilin and raised him together. Xu Shilin studied very hard, and one day, he achieved the top score in the imperial examination.

Dressed in official robes, Xu Shilin returned home, and went to the pagoda to visit his mother.

Kneeling before the pagoda, the young man hung the emperor's official hat, which had a flower hairpin, on the sago palm tree. Now, Xu Shilin knew that the hat was a symbol of the tree in blossom, and that it had special powers. The Leifeng Pagoda cracked open – the white snake-woman was finally freed and was joyfully reunited with her family.

Nian and the Spring Festival

There was once a creature called Nian – a fearsome-looking being with four sturdy legs, four imposing horns, and many sharp teeth.

Nian used to roam freely on the vast open plains. But as the human population grew and villages expanded, the creature had to retreat to more remote mountainous areas.

During the harsh winters, when food was scarce due to heavy snowfall, Nian would venture into the villages in search of food. On seeing this huge monster approach, the people were terrified.

To make matters worse, Nian's voice was nothing but a loud roar and nobody could understand what it was saying.

Their hearts would race as Nian drew near – they did not understand that the creature was simply in search of food to survive.

Desperate for relief, the villagers turned to the Kitchen God, protector of people's hearths and homes.

The people lit their stoves and produced smoke to send prayers up to the Kitchen God, asking him for help.

The Kitchen God listened to the people's plight and asked the Jade Emperor what could be done. The Emperor advised him to converse with the Nian monster and taught him the language of Nian.

Finally, the Kitchen God descended to earth carrying a magical, crimson silk ribbon with him.

The people greeted the Kitchen God's arrival with cries of hopeful happiness, and welcomed him with open arms.

The Kitchen God wasted no time. He approached Nian and posed two questions: "Why stray from your own abode? Why resort to harming people and their animals?"

Nian was grateful to have met someone who could converse in his tongue. He began to speak, "In the grip of icy winter, when my land ceased to yield nourishment, I journeyed here to seek food."

The villagers were astonished to hear these words and finally they understood.

They saw that this huge, scary-looking monster was in fact quite harmless. His ferocity was at odds with his appearance. The people marvelled at how looks can be so deceptive.

The Kitchen God approached Nian.

Then the Kitchen God spoke gently to Nian. "Allow us to help you," he said. "We will provide food for you during these tough winter months. In return, may I ask that you return to your realm? Then, once winter is over and with the advent of spring, you shall find food aplenty." And so the villagers fed Nian.

Nian thanked everyone for their helpfulness and returned home.

Jubilation filled the streets. There was a triumphant parade at the start of a new Spring Festival, and a new year. The red silk ribbon inspired households to adorn their doors with vibrant red couplets, and firecrackers were set off to celebrate.

From that day forward, the dawn of the new lunar year was celebrated as "Xin Nian", which means "New Year".

Many households would keep their lanterns ablaze through the night, bidding farewell to the old year and welcoming in the new.

THE CHINESE ZODIAC

ANCIENT CHINESE CALENDAR

The Chinese zodiac is a calendar designed with twelve animals. Each animal represents one year in a repeating twelve-year cycle. People born in a particular year share the personality of that year's animal. According to an ancient Chinese legend, the order was decided by a race, with the rat coming first.

RAT

PERSONALITY: Popular, sensible, curious, adaptable, clever, and personable.
YEARS INCLUDE: 1996, 2008, 2020

OX

PERSONALITY: Patient, cautious, strong-willed, thoughtful, and hardworking.
YEARS INCLUDE: 1997, 2009, 2021

TIGER

PERSONALITY: Frank, virtuous, intelligent, active, faithful, and expressive.
YEARS INCLUDE: 1998, 2010, 2022

RABBIT

PERSONALITY: Compassionate, friendly, sensitive, romantic, comforting, and modest.
YEARS INCLUDE: 1999, 2011, 2023

DRAGON

PERSONALITY: Energetic, ambitious, honourable, intellectual, excitable, and lively.
YEARS INCLUDE: 2000, 2012, 2024

TWELVE BRANCHES

The ancient Chinese created a calendar system for dates made up of twelve earthly branches. To make the branches easier to remember, each one was paired with an animal, which represented one year of the zodiac cycle.

SNAKE

PERSONALITY: Good-tempered, moral, passionate, gracious, determined, and wise.
YEARS INCLUDE: 2001, 2013, 2025

HORSE

PERSONALITY: Cheerful, clever, kind, likeable, adventurous, perceptive, and talented.
YEARS INCLUDE: 2002, 2014, 2026

GOAT

PERSONALITY: Quiet, wise, tender, sensitive, cautious, compassionate, and gentle.
YEARS INCLUDE: 1991, 2003, 2015.

MONKEY

PERSONALITY: Lively, sociable, sporty, flexible, quick-witted, practical, and creative.
YEARS INCLUDE: 1992, 2004, 2016

ROOSTER

PERSONALITY: Capable, clever, ambitious, warm-hearted, busy, and independent.
YEARS INCLUDE: 1993, 2005, 2017

DOG

PERSONALITY: Faithful, stubborn, straightforward, patient, kind, and trustworthy.
YEARS INCLUDE: 1994, 2006, 2018

PIG

PERSONALITY: Calm, strong, honest, tolerant, optimistic, light-hearted, and generous.
YEARS INCLUDE: 1995, 2007, 2019

How the Chinese Zodiac Began

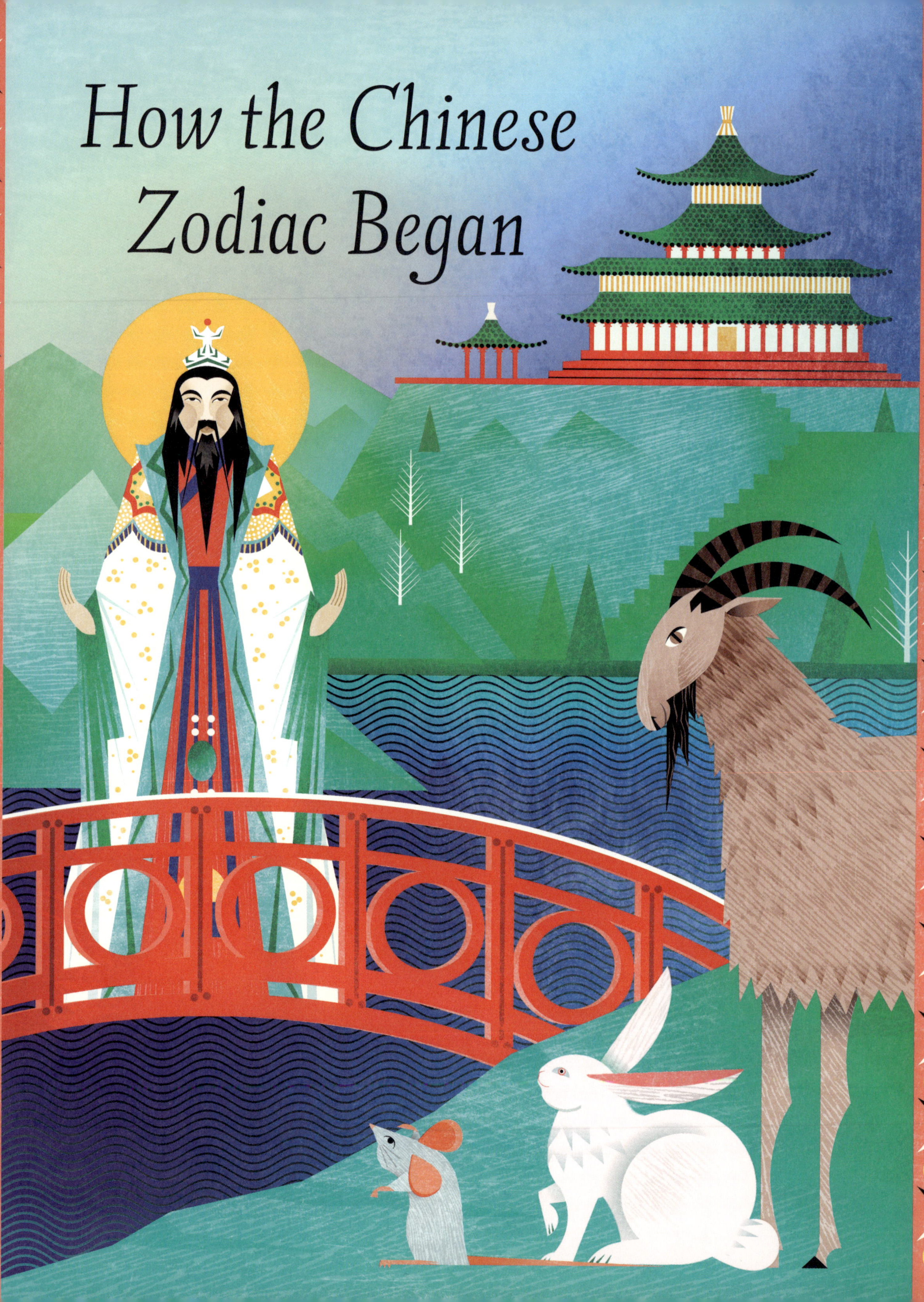

In the beginning, just after a time of chaos, there were twelve earthly branches that were established to measure time, which grew out from the heavenly stems.

The Jade Emperor wanted to select twelve animals to represent the twelve years that were linked with the twelve earthly branches. He felt this would make it easier for people to remember the years.

So the Jade Emperor issued a decree summoning all the animals in the world, informing them that the first twelve animals to arrive at the Emperor's palace on the day of the summer solstice would be the winners.

To reach the palace, the animals had to cross a plain, traverse a wide river, and climb over a tall mountain.

At that time, the Cat and the Rat were not just neighbours, but also close friends. Both of them wanted to take part in the competition. The Cat said, "We need to wake up early to get there first. However, I tend to oversleep, and may struggle to wake up in time. Please call me so we can go together." The Rat agreed to this plan.

However, on the morning of the summer solstice, the Rat woke up feeling anxious about being late. The little creature dashed off hastily, forgetting about the promise he had made to his good friend.

The Ox, aware of his slow pace, thought, "Even though I move slowly, as long as I get an early start, I shall definitely ensure myself a spot." On his journey, the Rat spotted the Ox and proposed, "Let me ride on your neck. I'll keep you company and sing songs along the way." The Ox agreed with a nod. Thus, the Ox carried the Rat, who sang as they travelled, "Brother Ox, cross the river, climb the hill."

The Rat's singing delighted the Ox, urging him to move faster with all his strength. When they reached the registration site, no other animals were in sight. Brimming with joy, the Ox bellowed, "We got it!" Just then, the Rat leaped off the Ox's neck but, without meaning to, jumped over the Ox and arrived first, while the Ox came in second.

The Tiger, renowned for its strength, was a born leader.

It thought that it would go in front of the other animals, testing the path so that others could follow its steps to avoid traps and dead ends. Therefore, it crossed ditches and overcame many difficulties and managed to secure third position.

Thanks to the tiger's adventures, the Rabbit avoided many potential dangers and difficult paths. Though timid, the Rabbit was remarkably hardworking. Its cautious nature, driven by attention to detail, allowed it to conquer various challenges, leading to its fourth place.

Following was the Dragon, the most capable among all animals, yet it arrived fifth.

Curious, the Jade Emperor inquired why it was not the first. The Dragon said, "I am responsible for bringing rain. Many places have been facing drought recently, and I finished ensuring rain in the southern regions before hurrying here. While this race is important to me, delaying the rain could have led to crop failure, causing much suffering among the people." Here, the dragon showed his thoughtfulness, though he was also rather pompous.

The Snake, shrouded in mystery, wished to be helpful like the Dragon. Despite lacking legs and the ability to fly, the Snake persevered on its journey. On land, it moved faster than a Rat through its agile twisting, and in water, it swam with the grace of a fish. And so, inspired by the Dragon, the Snake secured the sixth position through its great determination.

Some time later, the sound of hooves and the sight of dust rising from the road drew everyone's attention. The Horse was galloping with all its strength. It possessed remarkable skills on the road, and it could even swim in challenging waters. However, climbing hills proved to be very difficult. So the Horse had to be satisfied with seventh position.

Soon, the Goat, Monkey, and Rooster arrived.

The Jade Emperor asked, "Why are you three together?"

The Monkey replied, "We're well aware that we're just ordinary animals. The Goat can navigate rocky mountains, and I can swing through trees and run swiftly. The Rooster can fly and jump. However, the three of us can't swim. Then the Goat had a great idea and asked us to find a big, flat piece of wood, and this helped us."

The three friends had used the piece of wood as a floating raft so that they could cross the river safely. Now, the Rooster was a good and clear thinker and excelled at managing time. He organized the other two animals and made sure they paddled accurately and efficiently.

"And so it was good honest teamwork that helped us," said the Monkey.

The Rooster added, "Since the idea of using the wood as a raft came from the Goat, it should go ahead. The Monkey should be in front of me – just look at how energetically he paddled, with his bottom turning red and swollen." So, the Goat became the eighth, the Monkey the ninth, and the Rooster secured the tenth position.

The Dog, deeply loyal, wanted to be fair and just. Despite its eagerness to start, it had to do its duty of guarding the home until people woke up, so it left late and eventually secured eleventh position.

With only one spot left in the zodiac, everyone looked into the distance.

The Pig arrived, sweaty and breathless. Although the Pig was bulky and slow, it persevered, rejecting temptations and obstacles to finally make it onto the list. However, the journey left it exhausted and hungry, which gave it an insatiable appetite.

Meanwhile, the Cat arrived too late to be included. The selection was already over. From then on, the Cat became the arch enemy of the Rat.

Bole and the Thousand-Mile Horse

There was once an extraordinary horse that could travel a thousand miles in a single day.

Sadly, the horse lost its owner during a fierce battle and found itself wandering in the wilderness. Eventually, a man caught the magnificent steed and brought it to the market to be sold. Due to its impressive size, a farmer paid a higher price than was usual for an ordinary horse.

The farmer instructed the horse to plough the fields, but the thousand-mile horse had no knowledge of farming. When asked to carry goods to the market, it could not carry as much as expected. Frustrated, the man resorted to whipping the horse, causing it to wail in pain.

Eventually, the farmer decided to sell the horse.

This time, a horse trainer bought it. However, this new owner only provided the thousand-mile horse with the same feed as ordinary horses, leaving it hungry and weak, unable to run as fast as before. The man sighed and said, "I've bought many horses and trained them, but I've never encountered a thousand-mile horse as this one is thought to be. I now doubt that there are such beasts in the world!"

It so happened that the great Emperor Chu tasked his groom, Bole,

to find him a swift horse. So Bole set off on his mission. He journeyed far and wide and eventually came across the thousand-mile horse.

The horse stared straight at Bole, who cried out,
"This is indeed a thousand-mile horse!"

So Bole bought the animal, but when he brought the weakened, skinny creature before the Emperor Chu, and proclaimed him as a thousand-mile horse, the Emperor was not convinced.

Bole explained that to fully nurture its talents and abilities, its owner must understand how to feed it. Then Bole asked the Emperor, "Is it that there are no thousand-mile horses in the world, or it is just that there are no people that can recognize a thousand-mile horse?"

So, with the Emperor's consent, Bole took good care of the horse and fed it well. Soon the horse regained his strength and Emperor Chu was delighted with his new steed and treasured it.

And so the horse was left to gallop freely and happily through fields and plains for a thousand miles each day.

JOURNEYS AND ADVENTURES

Life is a journey. Some prefer a peaceful journey, others thrive on excitement. Some endure hardships, others sail smoothly. There are many tales of adventure in Chinese mythology, in which characters overcome obstacles to reach their destination.

Take, for example, Sun Wukong, who uses his cleverness, combat skills, and magic to protect his master and fellow disciples from countless perils. And there are the Eight Immortals, who each use their own unique ability to cross the East Sea.

Sun Wukong Causes Havoc in Heaven

In ancient times, on the Mountain of Flowers and Fruit in China, a magical rock was exposed to the heavenly energy of the sun and the earthly energy of the moon.

Inside the rock, a monkey was formed. This creature grew to be uniquely intelligent, agile, and hardworking. Soon, he was leading a group of monkeys, and he became known as the Monkey King.

One day, the death of an elder monkey made the Monkey King realize that life's existence is not permanent. Another wise monkey told him about a Taoist immortal, Master Puti Zushi, who could teach him incredible skills and knowledge. Intrigued, the Monkey King decided to embark on a quest to find this legendary teacher.

Under Puti Zushi's guidance, the Monkey King learned quickly, and proved himself to be an exceptional student.

He mastered various magical arts and gained the power to transform into seventy-two different forms. Impressed by the monkey's abilities, Puti Zushi gave him the name Sun Wukong, which means "awakened to the void", reflecting his wisdom and spirituality.

Returning to the Mountain of Flowers and Fruit, Sun Wukong travelled to the undersea realm ruled by the East Sea Dragon King in search of a weapon. The monkey challenged the dragon guards and warriors, causing havoc in the Dragon Palace, and finally

obtained a magical rod called Ruyi Jingu Bang, which could change its size according to his will.

The monkey then travelled to the Underworld and removed his name from the Book of Life and Death, seeking to achieve immortality.

Sun Wukong's behaviour greatly angered the gods. Some wanted to capture him, but others argued that it was better to keep him on their side. Finally, it was agreed that Sun Wukong should be offered the position of Keeper of the Heavenly Horses.

At first, Sun Wukong enjoyed the job. But on learning that this was a low-ranking position, he felt undervalued. He upped and left, returning to his mountain home.

The Jade Emperor and the other gods were furious. But they were well aware that the monkey's abilities could be of use to them. So, to tempt him back, the Jade Emperor agreed to give the Monkey King the title of Great Sage Equal to Heaven, and deceived him into thinking this was a position of high rank. Sun Wukong accepted, and was assigned the job of Guardian of the Peach Garden, allowing him to protect the sacred

Peaches of Immortality. This, the gods hoped, would keep him out of trouble. However, Sun Wukong was soon not happy with this either and once more rebelled.

Using his magical ability to cloud-travel, along with his powers of transformation, Sun Wukong entered the Heavenly Palace and confronted the Jade Emperor. He demanded to be recognized as an equal of the gods.

But this was a step too far. Fierce battles broke out between the monkey and the heavenly army. Sun Wukong was captured and imprisoned, and thrown into a fire stove belonging to the alchemist Laozi. But instead of being burnt to a cinder, Sun Wukong emerged with "Fiery Eyes and Golden Vision", which meant he could see far beyond what any mortal could.

Sun Wukong then used his powers to wreak havoc in the Heavenly Palace.

To put an end to the chaos, the Jade Emperor called upon the Buddha in the Western Heaven for assistance. The Buddha used his supreme powers to suppress the Monkey King and trapped him beneath the Five Elements Mountain to endure a long and painful punishment for his arrogance and defiance of divine authority. And there he remained for five hundred years.

SUN WUKONG

THE MONKEY KING

Sun Wukong is a mischievous monkey who causes trouble from the day he is born. He sprang from a magic stone that sat on the Mountain of Flowers and Fruit. He later becomes enlightened and uses his fighting skills, cleverness, and magical powers to protect his master and fellow disciples.

SACRED SYMBOLS

STONE
It is said that Sun Wukong was born from a stone that Nüwa used to mend heaven.

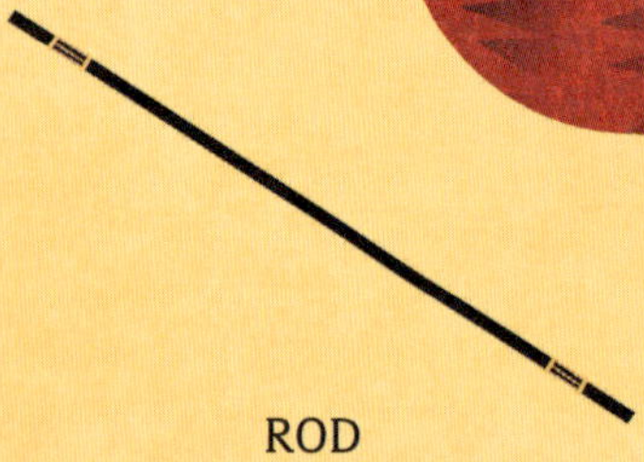

ROD
Sun Wukong carries a golden-banded rod that can change its size, fly, and attack opponents.

IMMORTALITY
Sun Wukong erased his name from the Book of Life and Death and so became immortal.

MARTIAL ARTS
Sun Wukong is a skilled fighter and a master of martial arts. He can transform himself at will into other creatures.

JOURNEY TO THE WEST

Together with the monk Tang Sanzang and two disciples, Sun Wukong travels westwards to India to find sacred Buddhist scriptures. On the way, they face demons and powerful gods, and encounter many moral dilemmas.

GOD

DRAGON KING

DRAGON GOD

The ferocious and powerful Dragon King is the Chinese god of water and weather. Also known as the Dragon God or the Dragon King of the East Sea, he commands the seas and oceans and decides when it should rain. He rules the other dragons, and all the creatures that live in oceans and seas.

SACRED SYMBOLS

WATER

The ruler of all bodies of water, the Dragon King governs lakes and rivers as well as seas and oceans.

SEASONS

Some say the Dragon King is linked with the changing seasons – spring, summer, autumn, and winter.

WEATHER

The Dragon King is a powerful weather god. He rules the skies and dispenses rainfall.

WELLS AND SPRINGS

The Dragon King is linked to all forms of water, including wells and springs.

FOUR DRAGON KINGS

Some sources say that there are four Dragon Kings, each in charge of a sea in a particular direction: East, West, North, and South. The Dragon King of the East Sea is the leader of the other three Dragon Kings.

Sun Wukong's Journey to the West

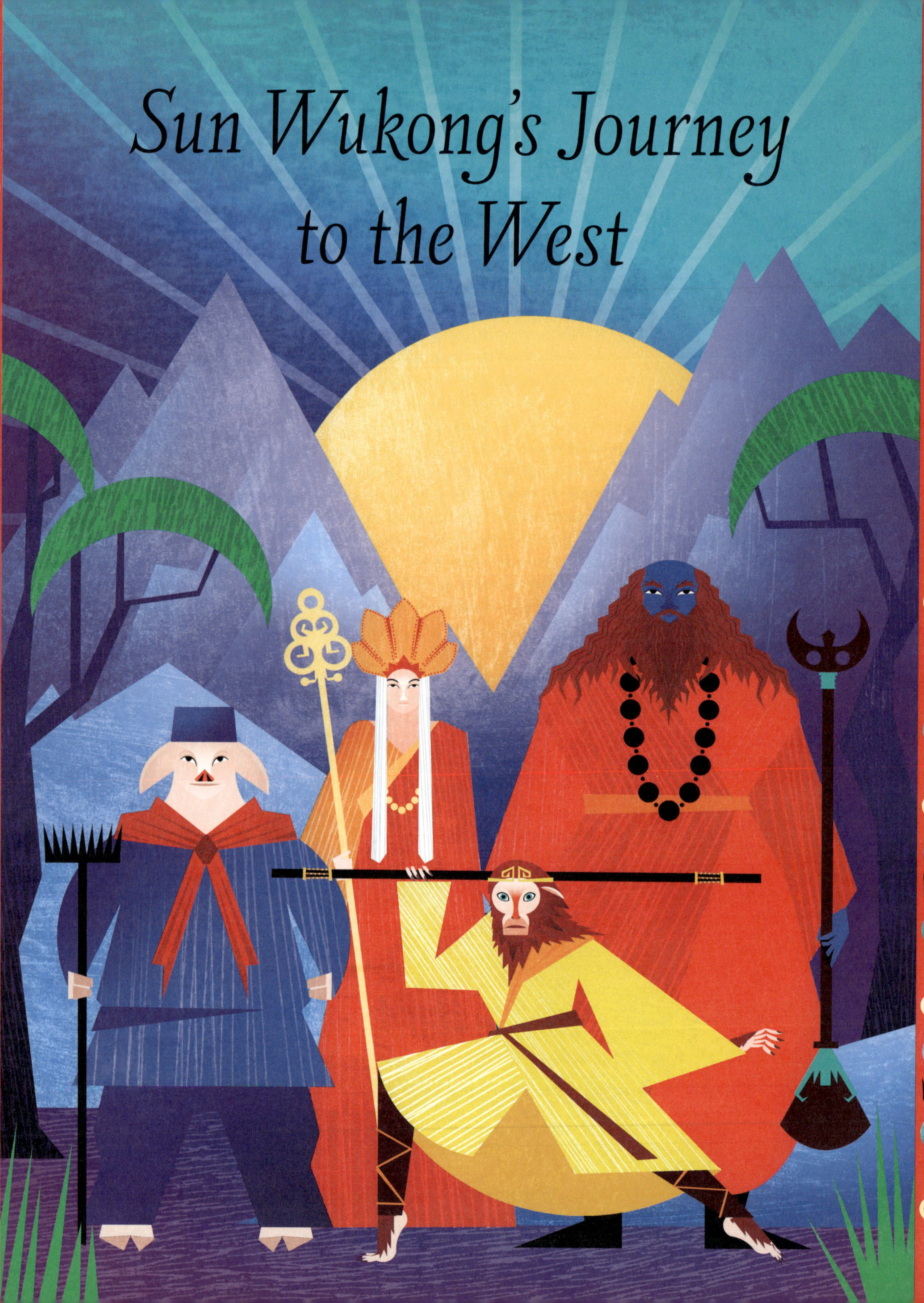

The Monkey King, Sun Wukong, was trapped underneath the Five Elements Mountain by the Buddha as a punishment for causing havoc in heaven.

During this time, Sun Wukong reflected on his actions. He started to learn about the value of humility and self-restraint.

About five hundred years later, a monk named Tang Sanzang was destined to embark on a perilous journey to the West to obtain sacred Buddhist scriptures.

Tang Sanzang had a pure heart and unyielding faith, but he knew his pilgrimage would be fraught with danger.

The Goddess of Mercy, Guanyin, convinced the Buddha to grant Sun Wukong a chance to redeem himself by allowing him to accompany and protect the monk Tang Sanzang on his journey to the West. So, Sun Wukong, along with two other disciples – Zhu Bajie, a pig-like creature with great strength and a huge appetite, and Sha Wujing, a reformed river demon – set off with Tang Sanzang on his journey.

Throughout their adventures, Sun Wukong used his cleverness, combat skills, and magic to protect his master and fellow disciples from countless perils. Along the way, they faced fierce demons, formidable gods, and challenging moral dilemmas. Here are two of their stories.

The Stealing of the Ginseng Fruits

Tang Sanzang and his disciples sought shelter at a temple. Here, two Taoist disciples treated Tang Sanzang with ginseng fruits.

However, Tang Sanzang mistook the ginseng fruits for babies and hesitated to eat them. But the pig-creature, Zhu Bajie, was tempted by the aroma of the divine fruits, and devoured several of them.

Encouraged by Zhu Bajie, Sun Wukong attempted to steal the fruits so they could all share them.

The two Taoist disciples scolded Sun Wukong for his greed. In a fit of anger, Sun Wukong knocked down the ginseng fruit tree and escaped, but was soon captured. Sun Wukong sought the help of the Goddess of Mercy, Guanyin, who revived the tree.

Sun Wukong now realized the value of the fruit and became friends with the master of the temple.

Three Strikes Against the White Bone Demon

When the monk Tang Sanzang and his disciples arrived at the White Bone Cave, the White Bone Demon sought to capture Tang Sanzang and attain immortality.

Firstly, the White Bone Demon used her enchanting magic to transform into a young village girl. As the monk approached her, Sun Wukong warned, "She's a demon, here to deceive you." With that, he struck the Bone Demon in the face with his rod. The "village girl" was killed, but the demon's soul escaped.

The demon then took the form of an old woman, pretending to search for her daughter. Sun Wukong recognized the demon once again and struck the "old woman". But the demon's soul escaped once more.

The demon transformed into an old man, heartbroken over losing his daughter and wife. "You may deceive others, but not me!" cried Sun Wukong. He struck out with his rod, but once more the demon escaped.

However, the monk Tang Sanzang thought Sun Wukong had killed innocent beings and expelled him.

Sun Wukong journeyed to the Mountain of Flowers and Fruit, where he finally caught up with his three travelling companions, who had been captured by the Bone Demon. Sun Wukong knew he had to prove his innocence and free his friends. He transformed into the Bone Demon's mother and encouraged the demon to show off her skills and transform once more into a village girl, an old woman, and an old man.

This finally revealed the demon's true monstrous form to the monk.

Tang Sanzang deeply regretted his misjudgement. He and his disciples joined forces with Sun Wukong once more. And in a fierce battle, they defeated the White Bone Demon and her demonic followers.

And so the monk and his three disciples journeyed on together, Sun Wukong's martial prowess and magical abilities helping to protect the group from various dangers. His wisdom and quick thinking often helped them navigate treacherous situations and overcome formidable adversaries.

Throughout their travels, Sun Wukong's bond with Tang Sanzang grew strong. He not only protected his master physically but also provided guidance and advice on their spiritual journey. They shared a unique teacher-disciple relationship, in which the monk's humility and compassion complemented the Monkey King's strength and wisdom.

Eventually, they reached the Western Heaven and obtained the sacred scriptures they sought.

The journey back to the East was arduous, but they overcame each obstacle through unity and mutual support.

Nezha Conquers the Dragon King

Long ago, the wife of General Li Jing from Chentang Pass was pregnant for an unusually long time of three years and six months.

When she finally gave birth, a flesh ball emerged. Li Jing used his sword to split it open, and a radiant light filled the room, revealing an adorable little boy born with two magical treasures – a gold bracelet and a fire-red sash. The great god and teacher, Taiyi Zhenren, named him Nezha, and took him on as his disciple.

As Nezha grew up, he became a righteous and courageous hero with exceptional intelligence.

Then a severe drought struck the land, and the people prayed for rain from the Dragon King – the ruler of the East Sea and of all dragons. However, the Dragon King demanded the sacrifice of children in return and sent his sea demons to seize them.

A terrible battle began. Armed with his magical gold bracelet and fire-red sash, Nezha defeated the demon soldiers, sending them back to the Dragon King's Crystal Palace.

The Dragon King was enraged. He sent his powerful third son, Ao Bing, to confront Nezha. But with the help of his two magical treasures, Nezha defeated and killed Ao Bing. Nezha did not stop at this. He journeyed to the Crystal Palace, captured the Dragon King, and made him promise to stop harming humans.

To this the Dragon King reluctantly agreed. Nezha returned home happily and told his father, "I've solved the problem, the Dragon King is not going to cause harm anymore." Li Jing was still worried, however.

Li Jing was right to be concerned. The Dragon King's promise was not to be trusted.

He gathered the other three Dragon Kings – who ruled the West, North, and South Seas – to seek revenge on Li Jing and Nezha. They raised massive waves and flooded Chentang Pass, demanding that Li Jing kill his son to stop the flood.

Lightning crackled overhead as torrential rain poured down, and Li Jing raised his sword, torn between his family's safety and the people's lives. His sword fell on the ground.

Seeing even bigger waves and knowing he could not defeat the four Dragon Kings, Nezha took up the sword himself, declaring, "I alone am responsible for my actions." With a heavy heart, he killed himself to protect everyone.

Satisfied, the Dragon Kings returned to their home under the sea.

The Divine Crane took Nezha's soul to the Golden Light Cave.

The Divine Crane took Nezha's soul to Mount Qianyuan's Golden Light Cave. The god Taiyi Zhenren, which means "perfected person", took lotus flowers, leaves, and tender roots from a lotus pond and arranged them into the shape of a person. The great god then cried, "Nezha, wake up!"

The flowers, leaves, and roots transformed back into Nezha. It was as if he had just woken from a long nap.

The god then gave him a new form of three heads and six arms, along with two magical treasures – the fire-tipped spear and two wind fire wheels for his feet.

Reborn with new weapons and new powers, Nezha charged into the Crystal Palace, capturing the four Dragon Kings and putting an end to their destructiveness.

From that day on, as well as wearing the gold bracelet and the fire-red sash, Nezha wielded the fire-tipped spear and travelled on the wind fire wheels to defend the human world. The Dragon Kings ceased their misdeeds, and peace and harmony returned to the land.

The Eight Immortals Cross the Sea

There were once Eight Immortals of Taoism. These mystical beings were different from many other deities, as they all originated from the mortal world and had their own flaws.

However, despite their imperfections, they shared a common passion for justice, righteousness, and the pursuit of enlightenment...

TIEGUAI LI

Tieguai Li, meaning "Iron crutch Li", had a limp and walked with the aid of an iron crutch. He often carried a gourd slung over his shoulder. Though Tie Guai Li appeared weak, his true power lay in his formidable skills.

ZHONGLI QUAN

The second Immortal was Zhongli Quan. He was often shown half-dressed, and cooled himself with a palm-leaf fan. Zhongli Quan had a carefree and leisurely manner, and was indifferent to the opinions of others.

ZHANG GUO LAO

Zhang Guo Lao was the eldest of the Immortals and knew the secret of long life. He rode a donkey backwards while travelling, spreading the teachings of Taoism. His donkey could travel a great distance during the day and fold up like paper at night, fitting into a small box. With just a mouthful of water, Zhang Guo Lao could revive his donkey for the next journey.

HE XIAN'GU

The only female Immortal was He Xian'gu. She was aware of the suffering in the mortal world and often travelled in the dry southern regions of China, bringing rain and getting rid of disease. Whenever good-hearted people prayed for her help, she appeared like a timely rain, granting them the ability to perform miracles.

LAN CAIHE

Lan Caihe was a wandering beggar, often dressed in tattered blue clothes with one foot in a boot and the other bare. Carrying a paddle drum, Lan Caihe wandered the streets singing songs, touching the hearts of listeners. Lan Caihe occasionally dressed in women's clothing, carrying a flower basket.

LÜ DONGBIN

On failing the imperial exam many times, Lü Dongbin left studying behind and roamed the world until attaining enlightenment. The most approachable of the Immortals, he was witty and loved people. He stood up for the oppressed and fought evil, all while enjoying wine and romance. A great swordsman, he could control his flying sword from a distance.

HAN XIANGZI

Han Xiangzi was taught the ideas of Taoism by Lü Dongbin. A talented musician, he often played the flute, and became the patron saint of flautists. As well as playing music, Han Xiangzi composed musical pieces. He often carried with him a basket of flowers and a jade flute.

CAO GUOJIU

Although enjoying a privileged status as the brother of an empress, the Eighth Immortal, Cao Guojiu, shunned a life of luxury and exploitation and embraced Taoist practices instead.
Cao Guojiu often wore a red official robe while holding a jade tablet.

The Eight Immortals hailed from eight different backgrounds and each had their own unique personality. Even after attaining immortality, many of their original characteristics remained, as their adventure to Penglai Island shows...

One day, the Eight Immortals were invited to a grand event on Penglai Island. Here, a great banquet of the Peaches of Immortality was to be held.

The Immortals prepared to cross the East Sea, but were confronted by ferocious waves. It was impossible to go by boat...

The Dragon King of the East Sea had taken a disliking to the Immortals and was determined to stop them crossing. So the Eight Immortals gathered together and discussed what they should do. Lü Dongbin – whom they all loved and would listen to because he was good and kind – suggested they each use their unique abilities to cross to the other side.

So it was that Tieguai Li used his gourd to float on the water, while Zhongli Quan tossed his giant palm-leaf fan into the sea, lying on it leisurely. Zhang Guo Lao

placed his paper donkey into the water, riding it backwards. He Xian'gu threw a vibrant red lotus flower into the waves, and balanced gracefully upon it. Lan Caihe held a flower basket and danced, while Lü Dongbin swung his sword to create a path, separating the water. Han Xiangzi played the flute, making the waves push him across to the other side, while Cao Guojiu used his jade tablet to part the waves.

Thus, the Eight Immortals used their unique talents to cross the sea.

Though each employed different approaches, they all achieved their common goal of reaching the other side. And so they joined together in the great banquet of the Peaches of Immortality and sang and danced all day and all night.

THE EIGHT IMMORTALS

LEGENDARY FIGURES OF TAOIST MYTH

The Eight Immortals are believed to have attained immortality through their practice of Taoism. They represent different genders, ages, and both financial and social statuses. As they were once mortals, ordinary people can relate to their different personalities. This makes them the most widely known Taoist figures in Chinese myth.

MOUNT PENGLAI

The Eight Immortals live on Mount Penglai, which is pure white. Its palaces are made from gold and silver, and jewels grow on the trees. There is no pain and no winter. There are rice bowls and wine glasses that are never empty and there are enchanted fruits that can heal any ailment, grant eternal youth, and resurrect the dead.

THE EIGHT IMMORTALS' TABLE

It is said that the Eight Immortals would sometimes sit together at the Eight Immortals' Table. This is a traditional piece of Chinese furniture that is square in shape. Each side can seat two people, making it ideal for the Eight Immortals to sit together.

SYMBOLS OF THE EIGHT IMMORTALS

Each of the Eight Immortals hail from a different background, including a royal family member, a beggar, and a Taoist priest. Each Immortal has its own distinct personality and represents a different social group: men and women, old and young, rich and poor, noble and lowly.

TIEGUAI LI

SYMBOL: Iron crutch; gourd
FEATURES: Lame; formidable skills
REPRESENTS: Inner spiritual development is more important than outward appearance

ZHONGLI QUAN

SYMBOL: Palm-leaf fan
FEATURES: Indifferent to others; carefree
REPRESENTS: A simple, carefree life is to be preferred to one of wealth and position

ZHANG GUO LAO

SYMBOL: Fish drum; donkey
FEATURES: Old age; has secret of long life
REPRESENTS: Avoid impulsiveness and consider things from all sides

HE XIAN'GU

SYMBOL: Lotus flower
FEATURES: Only female of the eight
REPRESENTS: Integrity, inner strength, feminine energy, and the ability to develop spiritually

LAN CAIHE

SYMBOL: Flower basket
FEATURES: Dressed in women's clothes
REPRESENTS: Embrace one's true self and be genuine, regardless of social norms

LÜ DONGBIN

SYMBOL: Flying sword
FEATURES: Scholar and warrior
REPRESENTS: Personal growth and spiritual change achieved through dedicated practice

HAN XIANGZI

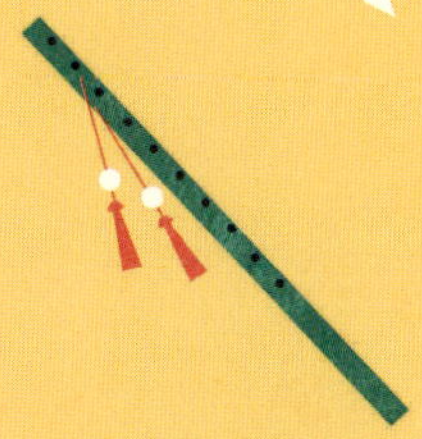

SYMBOL: Jade flute
FEATURES: Intelligent and good-looking
REPRESENTS: Artistic expression, a pure heart, and being in harmony with nature

CAO GUOJIU

SYMBOL: Jade tablet
FEATURES: Royalty; young brother of an empress
REPRESENTS: Serve the greater good and uphold justice in society

LOVE AND FRIENDSHIP

Love and friendship bind us together and bring joy to our lives. As these stories show, love isn't just about romantic desire, it is also about giving to others and staying committed.

The stories collected here explore relationships, social hierarchies, and matters of love and marriage. They also look at deep and lasting friendships. While some of these stories are very sad, they all celebrate the profound bonds of love and friendship as the foundations of our world.

The Weaver Girl and the Cowherd

Once upon a time in ancient China, nestling upon the riverbank of the Milky Way, there was a place where the realms of heaven and earth touched.

On the heaven side of the riverbank, there lived a young weaver girl called Zhinü, the daughter of the Queen of Heaven. As she gazed down upon the earth, a longing stirred within her. Zhinü found herself dreaming of exploring the mountains and valleys, and of diving into the sparkling rivers that flowed with stories untold.

Zhinü sighed, "How truly wonderful it would be if I could step upon the emerald earth, feeling the gentle touch of grass beneath my feet and the sweet caress of the wind upon my cheeks."

Meanwhile, on the earth side of the river bank, there lived a humble cowherd named Niulang.

As he watched his cows graze, he dreamed of soaring through the heavens like the birds that filled the sky.

Niulang sighed, "How truly wonderful it would be if I could be embraced by the light of the twinkling stars, and to be able to understand the wisdom that resided in the moon."

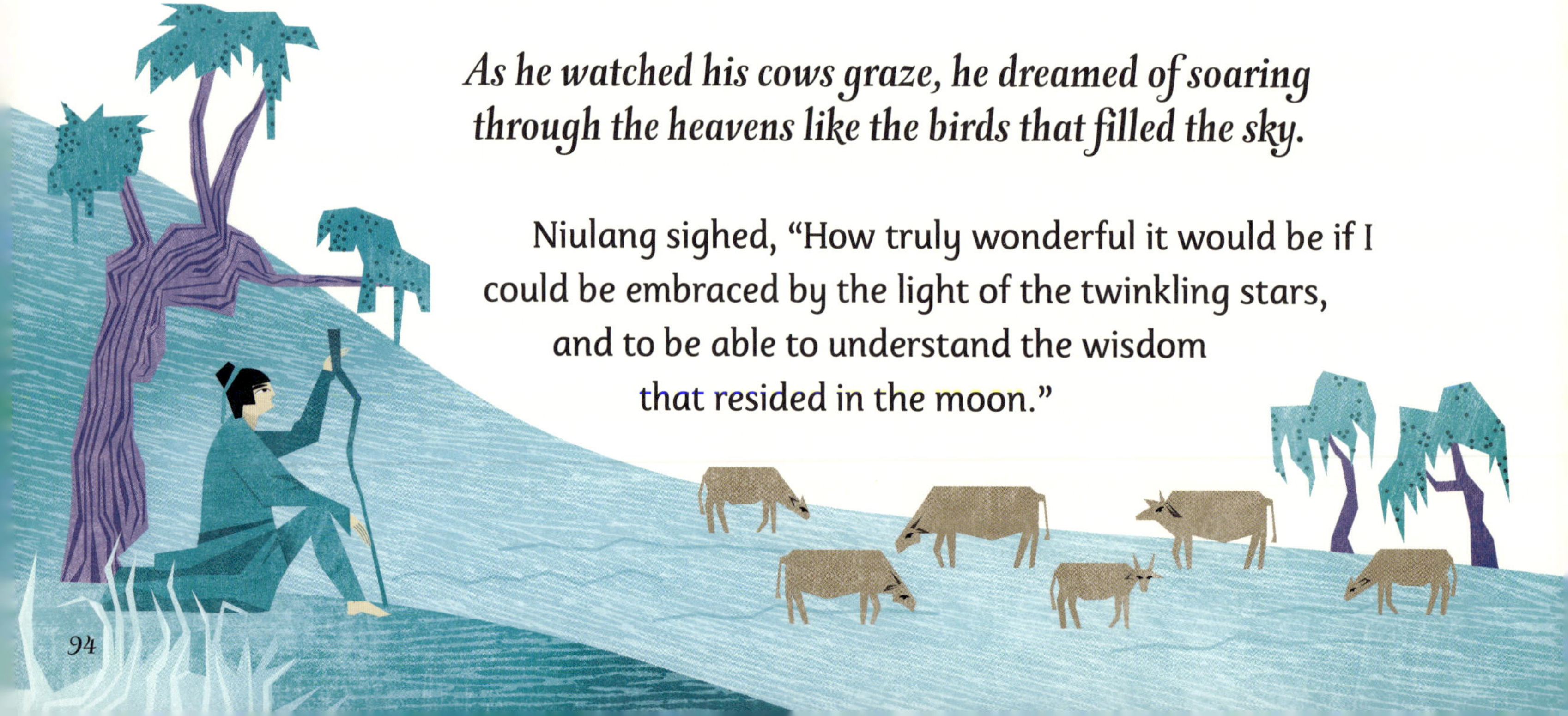

One day, Zhinü made a heartfelt plea to the Queen of Heaven, saying, "I humbly request your permission to descend to earth. I long to immerse myself in its vast wonders and to walk among its people." The compassionate Queen granted her request, permitting her to visit earth.

So one day, as the sun began its descent near a tranquil riverbank, Zhinü appeared.

As her feet touched the soft grass, the air seemed to hold its breath in awe. Not far away, Niulang couldn't believe his eyes when he saw Zhinü standing before him. Her beauty surpassed anything he had ever seen, and her voice was as sweet as a lullaby. They introduced themselves, and Niulang invited Zhinü to his house to have tea. From then on, Zhinü would visit Niulang whenever she had free time.

As they continued to spend precious moments in each other's company, Zhinü discovered in Niulang a compassionate and loving soul, while Niulang admired Zhinü's grace and wisdom. And so their hearts became intertwined.

Zhinü and Niulang made a home together, a sanctuary filled with warmth, laughter, and enchanting love.

Together, Zhinü and Niulang brought a daughter and a son into the world. Together, they created a harmonious blend of celestial magic and earthly simplicity. Zhinü and Niulang found a love that transcended the boundaries of heaven and earth. However, the celestial realm and the mortal world have distinct rules which Zhinü and Niulang had broken.

The Queen of Heaven decreed, "Though I recognize the depth of your love and passion, you must abide

by the laws of the celestial realm. Zhinü must return to heaven, and Niulang shall remain on earth to care for their children."

And so the couple were separated by the vast expanse of the river. Their love, however, refused to be extinguished, and their hearts longed for reunification.

The magpies of the sky witnessed the separation of Zhinü and Niulang, and were determined to help. However, their powers could only be harnessed on one day each year.

On the seventh day of the seventh lunar month, the magpies formed a bridge with their wings across the Milky Way that separated the celestial and mortal realms.

Now on that day each year, Zhinü and Niulang, along with their two children, walk across the Magpie Bridge. There, they embrace with their hearts overflowing with joy, and with their love shining brighter than any star in the sky.

ZHINÜ AND NIULANG

THE WEAVER GIRL AND THE COWHERD

Zhinü was a weaver girl who fell in love with a cowherd called Niulang. Tragically, they were separated, and could only meet once a year on the Magpie Bridge, which stretched across the Milky Way. Every year, on the seventh day of the seventh lunar month, a festival is held in China to celebrate this love story.

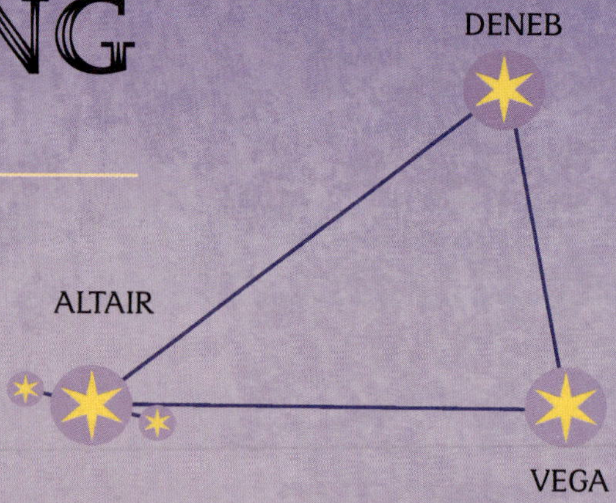

SUMMER TRIANGLE

There are three stars in the night sky that form a pattern called the Summer Triangle. It is said that the star Vega is Zhinü and the star Altair is Niulang. Deneb is the brightest star of all three, and this represents the Magpie Bridge.

There are two fainter stars near to Altair that are said to be the couple's two children.

QIXI FESTIVAL

The Qixi Festival, also called Chinese Valentine's Day, is held in China to celebrate the story of Zhinü and Niulang. Women may dress in traditional costume, called *hanfu*. People prepare offerings of tea, wine, flowers, and fruits and ask Zhinü and Niluang to answer their wishes.

Festival-goers eat a sweet pastry called *qiaoguo*. It is said that this will help reunite the couple on the Magpie Bridge.

MAGPIES

Magpies are considered lucky birds in Chinese culture and are often associated with joy, kindness, and love. In the story of Zhinü and Niulang, the Magpie Bridge symbolizes the unity of the heavens and the earth, and the meeting point of two souls in love.

Magpies appear in traditional Chinese art, poetry, and literature and are often featured in paintings, ceramics, and textiles.

Lady Meng Jiang and the Great Wall

Long ago, during the time of the First Emperor of Qin, there lived a beautiful woman called Lady Meng Jiang.

She fell in love with a young man called Fan Xiliang, as he did with her. They were soon married, and they were very happy together. But not long after their marriage, Fan was taken away by officials to work on the construction of the Great Wall.

As winter arrived, news kept coming from the north about the countless labourers freezing and starving to death while working on the wall. Lady Meng Jiang couldn't bear worrying any longer. She decided to make some warm clothes for her husband and set off to find him.

Lady Meng Jiang headed north. She crossed mountains and rivers while surviving on meagre provisions of steamed bread and cold water, and she rested whenever her legs grew weary.

On the first day of the tenth lunar month, Meng Jiang finally reached the Great Wall.

She asked the workers if they knew where Fan Xiliang was, and with tears in their eyes, they told her that he had died from exhaustion the previous month and that his body had been buried inside the Great Wall.

Hearing this devastating news, Meng Jiang pounded the Great Wall and burst into tears. Her cries were so loud that the sun and moon lost their radiance, and the sky turned dark. Her sobbing echoed through the autumn wind, and the ocean waves surged in response. Many labourers also shed tears, mourning Fan Xiliang's death.

Suddenly, there was a loud rumble, and a large section of the Great Wall collapsed, revealing a corpse. It was Fan Xiliang. Meng Jiang rushed forward, holding her husband's lifeless body and crying even harder.

At that moment, the Emperor of Qin and his entourage were passing by while inspecting the border walls.

Upon hearing that Meng Jiang had caused part of the Great Wall to collapse, he intended to punish her. However, when he saw how lovely she was, he wanted to make her his own. Meng Jiang couldn't bear the thought of being with him and wished she could die right then and there. Yet she thought of her husband's unavenged death and the grievances of the people. She held back her anger and asked the Emperor to hold a ceremony in honour of Fan and the many other labourers who had died.

Thinking that Lady Meng Jiang would then be his, the Emperor agreed to her request.

During the ceremony, the Emperor pretended to pay homage to the people who had died. But Lady Meng Jiang knew that this was false.

The grieving widow held her husband's remains close to her, and jumped into the sea, so that they could be together.

Later, in the place where Meng Jiang had leaped into the sea, people built a temple in her honour. To this day, the people of northern China commemorate Meng Jiang's journey and arrival at the Great Wall on the first day of October. The day is known as the Cold Clothes Festival, which is considered a festival for ancestral worship.

The Butterfly Lovers

Long ago, there was a young woman called Zhu Yingtai who had a passion for poetry and literature.

Yingtai yearned to pursue her studies outside her home in Shangyu County, near Shaoxing. However, at that time, it was not acceptable for women to be seen in public. Finally, her parents agreed to her leaving home, as they wanted their daughter to be happy. Yingtai decided to disguise herself as a young man to protect herself, and set off to Shaoxing.

On her journey, she encountered a scholar called Liang Shanbo who came from Kuaji, in Zhejiang.

After some talking, the pair found themselves sharing common values and realized that they truly understood each other. They swore an oath of brotherhood at the Grass Bridge Pavilion by scooping soil to make an incense burner.

From then on, they studied together, and formed a deep friendship. Yingtai fell deeply in love with Shanbo. However, Shanbo remained unaware of Yingtai's true identity, only thinking of her as a dear friend and brother.

Time passed. Yingtai's parents missed her and wanted her to return home. Yingtai loved her parents and knew she must journey to see them.

Tearfully, Yintai told Shanbo that she was going home and that she was not sure when they would see each other again. Upon parting, Yingtai tried to express her feelings of love through subtle gestures, but though Shanbo didn't understand her intentions, he promised to visit her soon.

So Shanbo visited Yingtai in her home, and there he discovered that his close friend of three years was, in fact, a young woman.

Shanbo was overwhelmed with emotion, and wanted to propose marriage to Yingtai at once. However, the young woman had already been promised to Ma Wencai, the son of a county magistrate. Now, Ma Wencai loved Yingtai, but she did not return those feelings. There was only room for Shanbo in Yingtai's heart. However, at that time, arranged marriage was common and free love was not allowed. The Ma family was powerful, and Yingtai's parents, though they guessed their daughter's true feelings, dared not refuse.

Knowing that they could not be together, Shanbo and Yingtai were forced to bid each other a tearful farewell.

Soon after, Shanbo passed the imperial examination and was himself to become a county magistrate. However, his sorrow at not being with Yingtai took a toll on his health, and he passed away.

On her wedding day to Ma Wencai, Yingtai made a detour to visit Shanbo's grave.

Overwhelmed with grief, she offered her prayers and felt overcome with intense emotion. Suddenly, the earth trembled, the tomb cracked open, and Yingtai leaped into the grave. The tomb closed again, and the storm subsided, leaving behind a rainbow suspended in the sky. Then Shanbo and Yingtai transformed into a pair of butterflies, and flew off together, departing from the mortal world to the heavenly sky in the sunshine.

Qu Yuan and the Dragon Boat Festival

Long ago, China was divided into many states that were constantly fighting – so much so that this time became known as the Warring States period.

At this time, one wise and highly ranked minister called Qu Yuan lived in the state of Chu, and this state enjoyed a peaceful alliance with another state, called Qi.

Zhang Yi was the prime minister of a third state, called Qin, and he was fearful about this treaty. He sent word to the King of Chu saying they were willing to give him six-hundred miles of territory if he would agree to break up the agreement. Now, Qu Yuan was worried about this, as he knew it would disturb the peace. However, the King of Chu was greedy for more land, so he agreed to break the alliance.

Months passed, and finally the ambassador of Chu met the Qin prime minister, Zhang Yi, to conduct the promised handover of territory.

Zhang Yi announced shamelessly, "This six-mile territory is ready to be handed over."

The ambassador was furious. He exclaimed,

"But wasn't it agreed upon as a six hundred-mile territory?"

To which Zhang Yi sneakily replied, "You must have misunderstood!"

On hearing the news that he had been deceived, the King of Chu immediately launched an attack against Qin. But without their former alliance they were now weaker and Chu suffered a heavy defeat.

The minister Qu Yuan, witnessing the invasion of his homeland, couldn't bear to abandon his state.

On the fifth day of the fifth lunar month, Qu Yuan embraced a rock and jumped into the Miluo River, so ending his life.

Upon hearing the terrible news, local people rushed to the river and rowed out in boats to try and rescue him. Realizing that it was too late to save him, they threw rice dumplings into the river, so that the fish would eat them rather than Qu Yuan's body.

Ever since, people have dragon boat races and enjoy eating rice dumplings at the Dragon Boat Festival, which is celebrated each year to this very day.

Foolish Grandpa Removes the Mountains

Once upon a time, in a small village, there lived an old man called Foolish Grandpa who was close to ninety years old.

Right in front of Grandpa's house there stood two enormous mountains. It meant that Grandpa and his family had to make a huge detour every time they stepped outside. Two rivers, glistening and lively, flowed either side of the mountains. But, alas, their connection was blocked by the stubborn obstacle of the mountains. Foolish Grandpa gathered his wife and all the family for a meeting and proposed to move the mountains to make travelling easier and to create a canal that would connect the two rivers.

Surprisingly, his family wholeheartedly supported his vision, and they began to work.

However, as the grandchildren watched the hard work unfold, they couldn't help but ask, "Grandpa and Grandma, why don't we just move to a different place?

It would be much easier for us, and we wouldn't have to work so hard."

Grandma, with a loving smile, replied, "My dears, moving away might be simpler, but by removing the two mountains, we will make travelling much easier. This will not only benefit future generations but also unite people. It's not just about our village – it's also about encouraging trade, communication, and harmony among neighbouring communities."

And so they worked on. However, it was an incredibly challenging task. The mountains were mostly rock, and the people at that time did not have dynamite or heavy machinery. Armed only with hand drills and sheer determination, they continued their labour.

After a month of backbreaking work, the mountains appeared as immense as ever.

Another old man from the village, called Wise Elder, noticed Foolish Grandpa and his family toiling relentlessly. He couldn't help but mockingly remark, "You are so old – how can you possibly move these huge mountains?"

Undaunted, Foolish Grandpa replied, "Perhaps I can't move them, but my sons, grandsons, and all future generations can. And we won't give up."

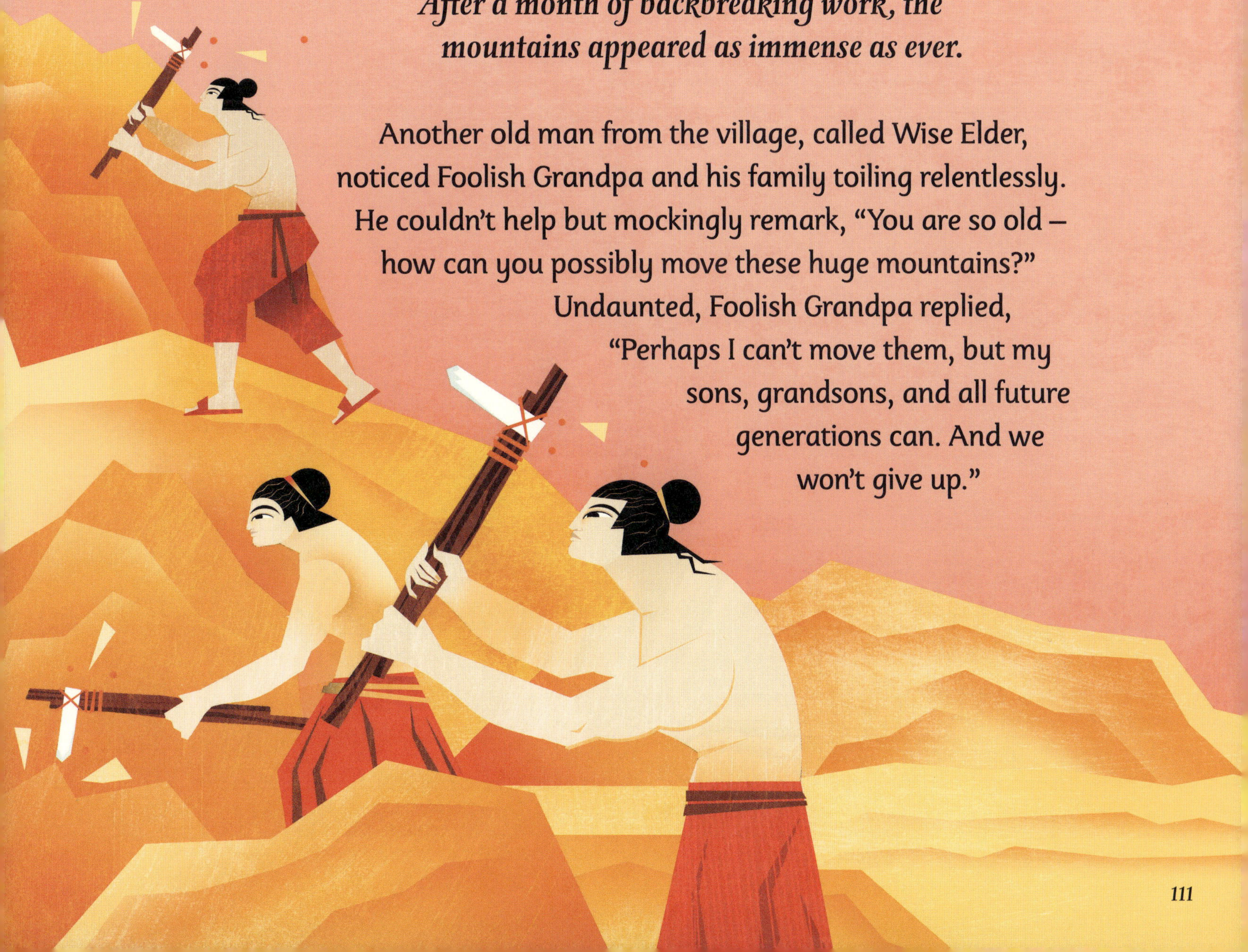

Even though the mockery stung, Foolish Grandpa and his family pressed on. As the adults continued chipping away at the mountains, the children played their part too, helping with cooking and gathering firewood. It was during one such moment that a young child accidentally spilled a pot of water on a heated rock they used to lay fire. To their astonishment, the rock cracked.

This new-found knowledge revolutionized their efforts.

Instead of laboriously chiselling and drilling, they now used fire to heat the rocks and then poured cold water over them, causing them to crack. This made everything so much easier, and the child's innocent discovery proved to be a turning point in the mountain-moving endeavour.

Soon, more and more villagers joined in the effort, inspired by the unwavering spirit of Foolish Grandpa's family.

The heavenly gods were impressed by the determined efforts of Foolish Grandpa and his family. So much so, that they sent two spirits to help them. Eventually, the mountains were moved and the two rivers were united by the canal.

Transport, trade, and communication flourished, and the village thrived like never before.

This tale was passed down through generations, inspiring countless souls with its message of perseverance, innovation, and the enduring belief that no mountain is insurmountable when hearts are united. And so too has the spirit of Foolish Grandpa, reminding us that great feats can be achieved through unity and determination.

Jiang Taigong Goes Fishing

Long ago, during the rule of the Shang Dynasty, the King of Shang governed with cruelty and tyranny, causing him to lose the support of his people.

At this time a man called Jiang Taigong, known for his mastery of military tactics, lived in seclusion near the Wei River in Shaanxi. Here, Jiang Taigong frequently went fishing by a creek.

While most people used bent hooks with bait to catch fish, Jiang Taigong used a hook that was straight and had no bait, dangling it high above the water's surface. As he raised his fishing rod, he would mumble, "Fish, if you wish, take the bait yourself!"

One day, a woodcutter arrived at the creek and scoffed at Jiang Taigong's unconventional fishing method, claiming that he would never catch a fish that way.

Taigong responded calmly, "I am not fishing to catch fish but rather to wait for a wise ruler to come and find me."

Meanwhile, King Wen of Zhou was planning to overthrow the Shang Dynasty, but lacked a skilled military planner to aid him in battle. When news of Jiang Taigong's peculiar fishing technique reached him, he was intrigued and sent a soldier to invite Taigong to his court. However, the fisherman ignored the soldier's request and continued to fish, at the same time repeating, "Fishing, fishing, if the big fish won't bite, the small fish don't stir."

Undeterred, King Wen realized that Jiang Taigong was a man of some importance, and decided to invite him personally. After talking with the fisherman, King Wen could see that Taigong possessed far-sightedness, vast knowledge, and expertise in many fields, including astronomy, geography, politics, and military affairs.

Jiang Taigong accurately analyzed the political situation and predicted the downfall of the Shang Dynasty.

He believed that a wise leader would rise to overthrow the tyrannical rule and establish a new dynasty for the welfare of the people. King Wen was deeply moved by Jiang Taigong's words. He knew that the man before him was the sage he had been searching for. "Please come with us and help govern the country!" he cried, and he invited Taigong to return with him to the capital.

At King Wen's court, Taigong was appointed as chief military officer and later promoted to prime minister, overseeing the nation's politics and military affairs. He helped develop agriculture and military training, leading to the expansion of the Zhou tribe's influence, and this led eventually to the overthrowing of the Shang Dynasty.

The Friendship of Boya and Ziqi

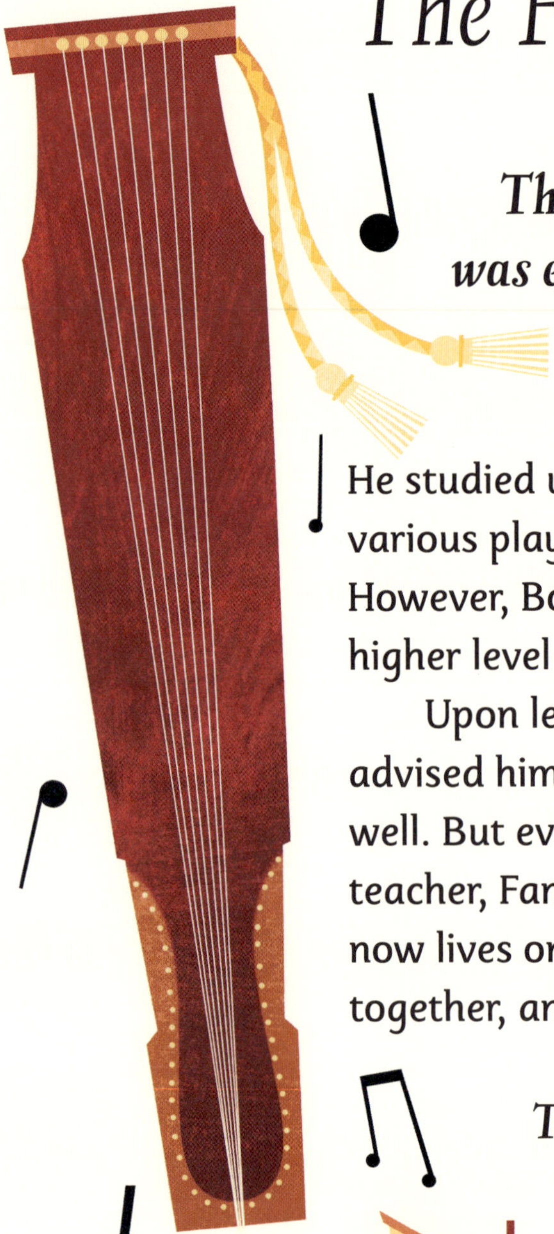

There once lived a man called Yü Boya who was exceptionally talented at playing an ancient stringed instrument, called a guqin.

He studied under the renowned teacher Cheng Lian, mastering various playing techniques and becoming a well-known musician. However, Boya often felt frustrated because he couldn't reach a higher level of artistic expression.

Upon learning about Boya's dilemma, his teacher Cheng Lian advised him, "I have taught you all my skills, and you have learned well. But even I haven't fully grasped the essence of music. My teacher, Fang Zichun, possessed a unique sensitivity to music. He now lives on an island in the East Sea. Let's pay him a visit together, and he might help you discover a new understanding."

Taking their provisions, the master and disciple set sail towards Penglai Mountain in the East Sea.

Once they arrived, Cheng Lian instructed Boya to stay and practise the guqin while he went to find Fang Zichun. As the boat departed, Boya found himself alone on the island, surrounded by the awe-inspiring beauty of nature.

Gazing at the vast sea with its turbulent waves and looking back at the tranquil mountains on the island, while listening to the sound of birdsong, he felt his spirit soar. Boya poured all his emotions into his music, skilfully expressing his feelings through the melodies he played.

Days passed, and Cheng Lian returned. After listening to Boya's performance, he said happily: "Now you are the best guqiner in the world!"

Boya now realized that nature was the best teacher, and his master agreed to let nature alone guide him.

The pair returned home. Boya found that he was a skilled composer as well as musician, and he became renowned for his talents. However, his music was complex and not always fully appreciated, making it difficult for him to find like-minded souls. So, despite his fame, Boya often felt lonely.

Time passed, and Boya decided to set off on a journey in nature once more. He arrived at the mouth of the Han River on a boat. However, due to the strong winds and waves, he had to anchor the boat near a small mountain.

As the wind and waves gradually subsided, and the clouds dispersed to reveal the moon, Boya saw that this night, the moonlight was especially alluring. Boya's passion for playing the guqin surged, and he started to play. Boya was immersed in his music when he sensed an unusual vibration in the guqin's strings. Stepping outside, he spotted a man sitting by the trees on the shore.

The man explained, "Sir, please don't be alarmed. I am just a woodcutter passing by. Your guqin playing was so captivating that I couldn't help but stop and listen."

The woodcutter said his name was Zhong Ziqi, and he carried a bundle of firewood with him.

Boya was astonished that a mere woodcutter could appreciate the depth of his music. Yu Boya excelled in playing, while Zhong Ziqi was gifted in listening. When Boya thought of towering mountains, Ziqi remarked, "Wonderful! Your majestic and powerful music is like the towering Mount Tai standing right before me!" When Boya thought of flowing water, Zhong Ziqi responded, "Excellent! The refreshing and smooth sound is like the surging river flowing through my heart!" No matter what Boya thought about when playing, Zhong Ziqi understood perfectly.

Overwhelmed with joy, Boya knew that he had found his long-sought kindred spirit. They spent the night talking and playing music, realizing that their musical connection was unparalleled. But they felt that they had met each other too late and they made a pact to meet again at the same place the following year at the Mid-Autumn Festival.

The next year, Boya returned to the same place by the Han River, expecting to be reunited with Ziqi.

However, Ziqi never arrived. Boya played the guqin with great fervour, believing that Ziqi would hear the music and come.

Sadly, Boya later learned from a local elder that Ziqi had passed away. Before his death, Ziqi had left instructions to build his grave by the Han River to hear Boya's music.

Devastated by the loss of his dearest friend, Boya performed the piece "High Mountains and Flowing Waters" beside Ziqi's grave. When he finished playing, he broke the strings of his guqin, sighed deeply, and shattered the cherished instrument on a nearby rock. "Without my soulmate, to whom shall I play this guqin?" he cried.

The friendship between Boya and Ziqi has moved countless hearts throughout history. Even today, the term *zhiyin*, which means "knowing the music", is used to describe a deep connection and understanding between friends.

ABOUT THE MYTHS

The myths of ancient China have been retold and passed down for thousands of years. The early stories focused on the cosmos, the origins of humanity, and the relationship between humans and nature. As people's understanding of nature deepened and society evolved, later tales explored relationships, social hierarchies, and love and marriage.

These stories – old and new – represent the essence of China's heritage. And they help us to understand the unique flavour and diversity of Chinese civilization.

HUMAN STRENGTH AND INDEPENDENCE

Chinese myths quite often focus on humans and everyday life rather than gods and the heavens. Many stories were passed down to teach future generations about the importance of perseverance and strength. Over the years, this teaching has encouraged a spirit of resilience and self-reliance among Chinese people.

The story of Foolish Grandpa and the Mountains reminds us that great feats can be achieved through unity and determination.

EXPLORING THE MYTHS

The earliest written records of ancient Chinese myths can be traced back to about 3,000 years ago. There is no single collection of Chinese mythology from one period. The stories developed from many sources and have been retold and reinvented at different times. They are often a blend of historical events and both real and legendary characters.

LEARNING FROM OTHER CULTURES

China was separated from the rest of the world at first. Then, from around 130 BCE, it started to trade along the Silk Road. This helped open it up to exchanging ideas and stories with other cultures, such as in the legend of Sun Wukong.

In one of the stories of Sun Wukong, the monk Tang Sanzang journeys to India to obtain Buddhist scriptures.

WOMEN

Many stories feature women as central characters. Women often play active roles and set off on adventures, such as Leizu, who travels far to discover silk, and Lady Meng Jiang, who journeys across China in search of her husband.

In The Butterfly Lovers, Yingtai shows strength and purpose when she disguises herself as a boy so that she can journey away from home and pursue her studies.

DIFFERENT BELIEFS

Chinese myths contain ideas from different belief systems, especially Confucianism, Taoism, and Buddhism. This is most clearly reflected in the character of Sun Wukong in Journey to the West, which incorporates elements from all three faiths.

AGRICULTURE

Most Chinese people lived and worked off the land, and there are many stories in Chinese mythology that reflect this. The god of farming – Shennong – was greatly revered throughout ancient China. As well as inventing the plough, he travelled across the land and discovered grains such as rice, millet, and wheat.

DAILY LIFE

By reading Chinese mythology, we can gain a glimpse of how people lived in ancient China. Most people dwelt in villages and made their living from farming. As the empire developed, education and the arts flourished and many great advances were made, such as the invention of printing and a new ceramic material called porcelain.

FAMILY LIFE

In many homes, three generations of the same family lived together. The head of the household, usually the grandfather, lived with his wife and children, together with their children. Families obeyed strict rules and treated each other with respect. This was in line with the teachings of the great Chinese philosopher, Confucius.

Children were taught to obey their parents.

FARMING

Agriculture was central to life in China. The fertile land best suited for farming was found around the Yellow and the Yangzi rivers. Rice was grown in flooded paddy fields. Millet and wheat were also farmed.

The god Shennong is the father of agriculture and medicine.

CHINESE MEDICINE

Traditional Chinese medicine, which dates back more than 4,000 years, is based on using many herbal remedies alongside a balanced diet. Its practice combines ancient philosophy with practical skills.

Herbs such as ginseng, ginger, and five-flavour berry are among those used in Chinese medicine.

ARTS

Chinese people shared a love for the arts. Educated people were often skilled at specialized handwriting, called calligraphy, as well as poetry and painting. Music was important too. Two zither-like instruments, called *qin* and *se*, were popular.

The god Fuxi is credited with inventing the two string instruments, *qin* and *se*. He is also said to have invented calligraphy.

CRAFTWORK

The ancient Chinese were skilled craftworkers, making objects from materials like porcelain, jade, and bronze. Jade was prized for its strength and beauty. The jade-green colour was linked with immortality and heaven.

The Jade Emperor was named after this precious stone, a symbol of immortality.

CLOTHING

Clothing varied depending on whether you were rich or poor. Generally, peasant farmers wore loose garments made of hemp – a rough fabric woven from plant fibres. Emperors and members of the court wore splendid robes of fine silk.

The empress Leizu is said to have discovered silk farming, and invented the silk loom.

CHINESE BELIEFS

Over time, three main religions developed in China: Taoism, Confucianism, and Chinese Buddhism. Together, they became known as the "Three Ways". Aspects of these three faiths are found in the myths of China, such as in the stories of the Monkey King, Sun Wukong.

TAOISM

Many of the myths of ancient China are inspired by Taoism, which is both a religion and a philosophy. Taoism seeks a state of contentment, free from desires and worldly influences. It emphasizes the connection of humans with nature and encourages the pursuit of inner peace.

CONFUCIANISM

Confucianism is both a religion and a philosophy. It emphasizes personal development, family values, good governing, and social harmony. It stresses the importance of virtues such as kindness, loyalty, and sincerity. Over the years, Confucianism has had a profound influence on traditional Chinese society.

Confucianism is based on the thoughts of the philosopher Confucius (551–479 BCE). He taught the importance of showing respect to your parents and ancestors.

CHINESE BUDDHISM

Buddhism was introduced to China by monks from India in around 150 CE. The goal of this religion is to achieve full enlightenment, called Nirvana. This means to fully accept the impermanence of everything, and so break free from the cycle of life, death, and rebirth.

Chinese Buddhism shares links with Taoism. It is concerned with breaking free from the "wheel of life", or *bhavacakra*.

Laozi is the founding figure of Taoism. He embodies the concept of the Tao ("the Way") and emphasizes living in harmony with nature.

The idea of Yin and Yang is central to Taoism. Yin (dark, feminine) and Yang (light, masculine) are in everything in different proportions. Harmony is achieved by maintaining the balance between them.

In Confucianism, Tian is the force that guides the heavenly moral order. It is sometimes represented by a simple figure.

The founder of Buddhism, Shakyamuni Buddha is revered as the Enlightened One who achieved the highest state of wisdom and compassion. His teachings form the core of all Buddhist philosophy.

ANCESTOR WORSHIP

Ancient Chinese people had huge respect for their elders and placed great value on ancestor worship. Each home had a shrine that was used to honour ancestors. People brought gifts of food and drink to their temples to honour the spirits of their ancestors, and celebrations were held in remembrance.

SPRING FESTIVAL

Also known as the Chinese New Year, the Spring Festival is the most important festival in China. It falls on the first day of the lunar calendar, which varies between late January and mid-February. Families and friends unite in celebrations, which include dragon and lion dances and glorious firework displays.

QINGMING FESTIVAL

This festival is a time for paying respects to ancestors and remembering loved ones who have died. Also known as Ancestors Day, it takes place in early April. On this day, people visit the graves of their ancestors, give flowers and other offerings, and remember those who have passed away.

DRAGON BOAT FESTIVAL

This festival, held between late May and early June, is to commemorate the legendary poet Qu Yuan. The story goes that Qu Yuan once jumped into the Miluo River, and people rowed out to try and save him. From that day, people have held dragon boat races and eaten *zongzi* (sticky rice wraps) in his honour.

MID-AUTUMN FESTIVAL

Also known as the Moon Festival, this is a very important holiday in Chinese culture and is a time for celebrating the harvest. It falls around mid-September during the full moon. People get together with family and loved ones, eat mooncakes, hang up lanterns, and make offerings to the moon.

FESTIVALS OF CHINA

Since early times, festivals have been held all over China. They were a time for giving thanks to the spirits of nature, honouring ancestors, seeking blessings, and warding off evil. The festive holidays also helped strengthen bonds between families and society. A time for joy and celebration, the eight major festivals shown here are still held in China and many parts of the world today.

THE LANTERN FESTIVAL

Also known as Yuanxiao Festival, this falls between mid-February and early March. People hang up colourful lanterns, eat *tangyuan* (sweet rice flour dumplings), and enjoy solving lantern riddles – all to celebrate togetherness and happiness.

WINTER CLOTHING FESTIVAL

This holiday – also known as Han Yi Festival – marks the start of winter and falls in mid- to late November. On this day, people wear warm clothing to welcome the colder season and pray for health and safety during the winter months.

THE DOUBLE-NINTH FESTIVAL

This festival falls in mid- to late October. Also known as Chongyang Festival, this is a time for respecting and honouring the elderly. Activities include climbing mountains, appreciating chrysanthemum flowers, and wishing for peace and prosperity.

THE QIXI FESTIVAL

Otherwise known as Chinese Valentine's Day, this festival is held between August and early September. People exchange gifts, and make a wish for a happy marriage. It is based on the legend of Zhinü and Niulang, who are said to meet on this day on the Magpie Bridge.

IMMORTAL BEINGS

In Chinese mythology, there are many immortal beings. They vary in status from the Eight Immortals to the god and goddess at the top of the heavenly hierarchy – the Jade Emperor and Xiwangmu. Under this duo is a court of gods who act as servants and officials. These heavenly bureaucrats reflect the huge earthly civil service that existed in imperial China.

HEAVENLY RULERS

Rather than being portrayed as purely divine beings, Chinese gods and goddesses often have human-like qualities. Their stories and backgrounds are rich and varied, and everyone can relate to them. Each god or goddess is associated with different aspects of life.

The Jade Emperor is often seen as the supreme ruler of the universe. He is a force for good and presides over both heavenly and earthly matters.

Xiwangmu, or the Queen Mother of the West, is associated with immortality and longevity. She holds court in the mystical Mount Kunlun.

The Yellow Emperor, also called Huang Di, is a powerful, warlike god. His wife is Leizu, and she is credited with inventing silk farming.

CREATOR GODS

In Chinese mythology, there is no single, all-powerful creator god. The main god connected to the creation of the world is Pangu, while Nüwa, the goddess of humans, helped mend the sky and create people. Then her twin brother, the god Fuxi stepped in and formed society, making the rules that people could live by.

Pangu is the creator god who came from a cosmic egg. He separated the egg into Yin and Yang, the two opposite, yet connected, forces of the universe.

Nüwa is the mother of humanity and the twin sister of Fuxi. She was involved with the creation of heaven and earth and is the people's protector.

Fuxi is one of the first gods. He taught people the laws of nature and society. He developed the marriage system and promoted the arts – especially music.

The goddess Guanyin protects those in need, offering relief from suffering. She is linked to the Bodhisattva of Compassion, one of the most popular figures in Buddhism.

Suirenshi helped people live better lives through his discovery of fire, and by showing people how best to use it. He later became known as the God of Fire.

HELPFUL GODS

The gods were often called on to help people. There were gods who presided over health or looked after new mothers, and others who helped with exams or discovered things. There were also the "Three Star Gods": Fu, the god of happiness, Lu, the god of wealth, and Shou, the god of long life.

MESSENGER GODS

There were lesser gods who acted as intermediaries between gods and earth. The most popular of these was the Kitchen God. He was said to produce an annual report of every person's deeds and deliver it to the Jade Emperor.

Many Chinese homes had a portrait of the Kitchen God in their kitchens. At the end of the year, people smeared honey on the portrait to make the god's report "sweet". They then burnt the portrait in a stove, and the smoke was said to carry the report to the Jade Emperor.

THE EIGHT IMMORTALS

In Chinese myth, the Eight Immortals are a group of legendary immortal beings, or *xian*. Each being has its own symbol. Most of the Immortals are said to have been born in the Tang or Song Dynasty. They are revered by the Taoists.

OFFERINGS TO THE GODS

People often visited the temple to pray to the gods and make offerings. They used smoke from burning incense to send messages to heaven. People would choose a deity to suit their needs or prayed to a favourite god or goddess, such as Chang'e, the goddess of the moon.

THE GREAT PENG

There have been many interpretations of the story of the Great Peng – the mythical bird that flies high above the earth and all worldly concerns. One popular idea is that even if we achieve greatness, there might be even better possibilities to explore. It teaches us to dream big and always seek to journey beyond the present horizon.

THE CHINESE PHOENIX

The immortal Chinese Phoenix is not like any other phoenix. Also called Fenghuang, it represents both male and female, Yin and Yang. It is the symbol of the empress, just as the Chinese dragon symbolizes the emperor. Descriptions of Fenghuang vary, but it is thought that it had the splendid tail of a peacock.

The Great Peng is an ancient mythical creature, and appears in the ancient Taoist text, *Zhuangzi: Free and Easy Wandering.*

Fenghuang's birdsong is said to be very beautiful. In the story "The Chinese Phoenix and the Hundred Birds", Fenghuang is celebrated as the Bird King.

MYTHICAL CREATURES

Chinese myths are full of an amazing mix of creatures – many reflecting human traits and characteristics, while others carry god-like energies. They range from the majestic Great Peng, a mythical bird linked to Taoism, to the adorable Jade Rabbit who lives on the moon. Here are just some of the wonderful creatures that you'll find in the pages of this book.

CHINESE ZODIAC

The twelve-year cycle of the Chinese calendar is linked with twelve animals, and people born in a particular year share the personality of a certain animal. The story goes that the order of the animals was decided by a race between the animals, with the rat coming first.

DIVINE TURTLE

The divine turtle, or spirit turtle, is believed to represent long life in Chinese myth. In the story "How Nüwa Repaired the Sky", the Divine Turtle sacrifices its feet to support the four corners of the world.

THE JADE RABBIT

The Jade Rabbit lives on the moon mixing a potion – the elixir of life – that grants eternal life to whoever drinks it. Stories vary about the Jade Rabbit's origins. Some tales say the Rabbit was originally Yi, others say that Chang'e was changed into the Rabbit as a punishment for drinking the elixir.

THE WHITE SNAKE

There are many versions of the Legend of the White Snake, but the central plot remains the same: the White Snake transforms itself into a beautiful lady and marries a man called Xu Xian. Meanwhile, a green snake turns into a woman and becomes her friend. The legend is about the Taoist search for immortality, and the struggle between good and evil.

THOUSAND-MILE HORSE

The thousand-mile horse, also called Qianlima, is said to be too swift to be mounted by any human, and is helped by the wise horse trainer Bole. Since early times, the Qianlima was a metaphor for very talented people. The poet Han Yu said, "There must first be Bole, and then there will be a thousand-mile horse."

THE CHINESE DRAGON

Also called Long, the Chinese dragon is a symbol of power, strength, and good fortune. In myths, many dragons are a force for good. However, while the Dragon King who commanded the seas is benevolent in some stories, he is evil in others. As beings of great power, dragons are closely linked with the Chinese emperors.

ROYAL DRAGON

Dragons were a symbol of the divine power of the Chinese emperors. It was thought that the first emperors were born with birthmarks in the shape of a dragon. It was even believed that the emperors became dragons at the end of their reign.

The Chinese emperor's throne was called the "Dragon throne", and this name was also used to describe the monarchy itself.

The emperor's ceremonial robes were called dragon robes, or *longpao*, and were decorated with dragon symbols.

WINGLESS WONDER

Usually shown without wings, the Chinese dragon has the head of a crocodile. Its body is like that of a giant serpent with scales, its legs are short and stubby, and its feet have long, sharp claws.

Dragon King of the North

KINGS OF THE SEAS

According to some stories, there were four dragons of the seas who each had the title of "Dragon King". They could take on human form and transform into dragons. They ruled over four bodies of water that formed the boundaries to ancient China – the East, South, West, and North Seas.

Dragon King of the West

In some accounts, the Dragon King of the East rules over the other three Dragon Kings.

Dragon King of the East

Dragon King of the South

CHINESE PAINTINGS

Pictures of dragons in Chinese art go back thousands of years. Dragon images appear in paintings, sculptures, architecture, and craftwork, making it one of the iconic symbols of Chinese culture.

Red dragons were associated with the Ming Dynasty (1368–1644). Yellow and gold dragons were linked with the Qing Dynasty (1644–1912).

PRAYING FOR RAIN

Chinese dragons were associated with forces in the natural world, especially rainfall. Dragons, it was believed, had the power to make it rain. In times of drought, people would perform rituals and pray to the Chinese Dragon to make it rain.

MYTHICAL PLACES

Chinese mythology is steeped in stories about magical places. From the towering Mount Kunlun, home of the heavenly gods, to the mystical tree, Fusang, where the ten suns resided before they were shot down, the tales are rich in symbolism and mystery.

MOUNT KUNLUN

The mythical Mount Kunlun was the home of the gods, especially the Queen Mother of the West. Mount Kunlun was believed to be the centre of the universe where heaven and earth met. Like the real mountain range of the same name, it is said to lie in northwest China.

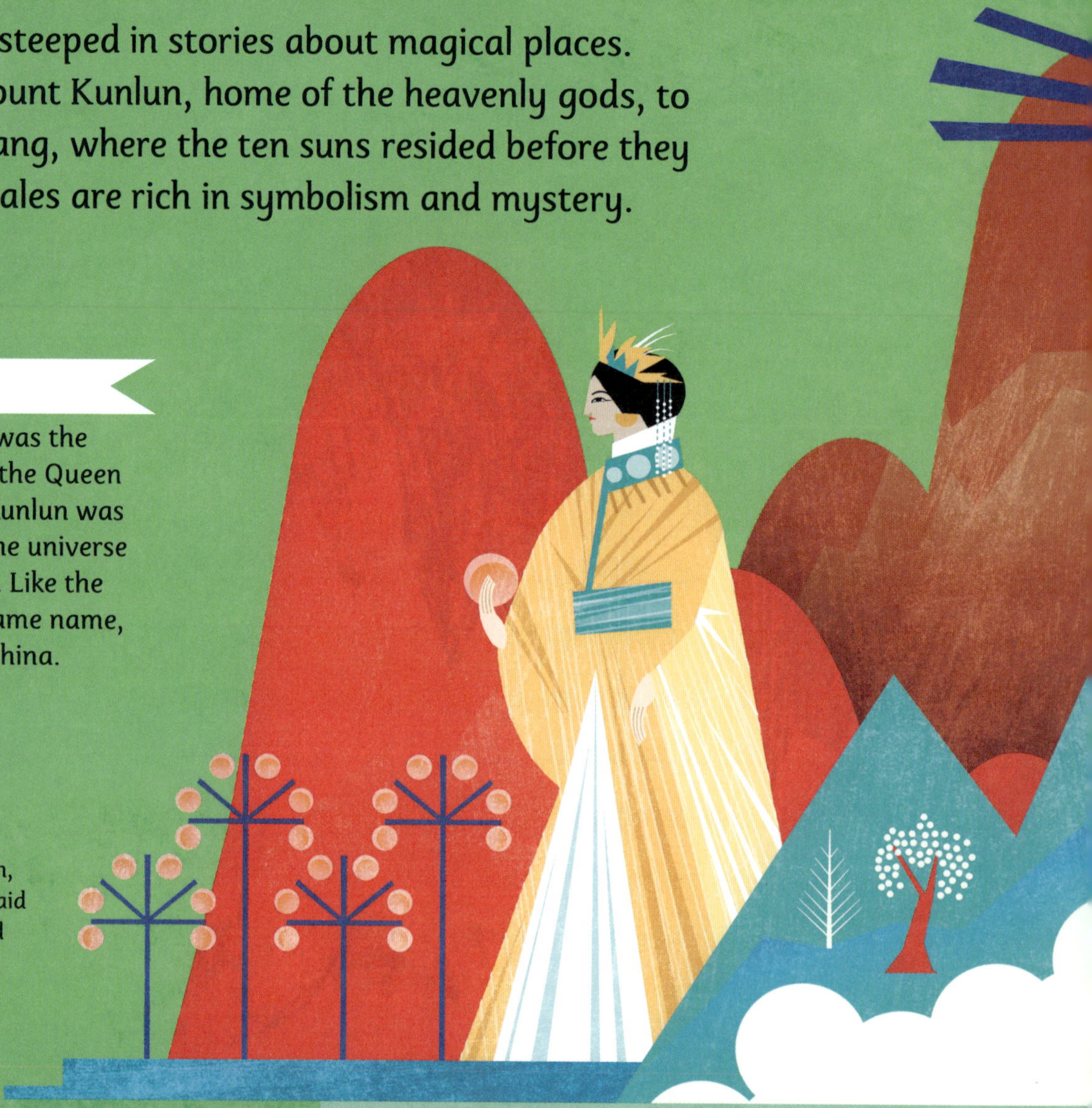

In the garden on Mount Kunlun, peach trees grow. Peaches are said to appear every few thousand years and give immortality to anyone who eats of the blessed fruit.

FUSANG

Fusang is the divine tree that stood on the shores of the East Sea. On it perched ten suns and ten three-legged crows. Later, Yi shot down nine of the suns from the sky.

MOUNTAIN OF FLOWERS AND FRUIT

Also called Mount Huaguo, the Mountain of Flowers and Fruit is a major feature in the novel *Journey to the West*. The Monkey King sprang out from inside the mountain.

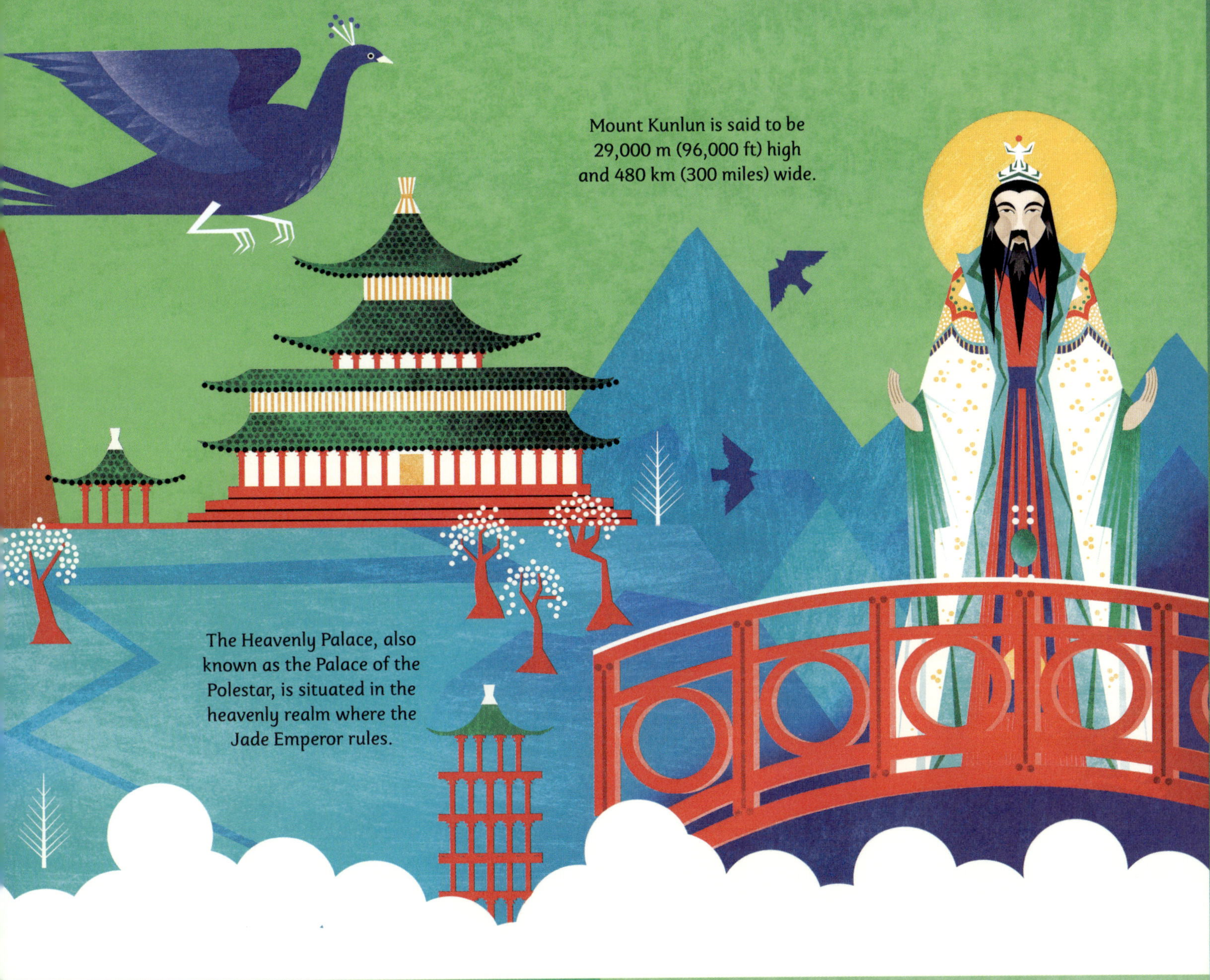

Mount Kunlun is said to be 29,000 m (96,000 ft) high and 480 km (300 miles) wide.

The Heavenly Palace, also known as the Palace of the Polestar, is situated in the heavenly realm where the Jade Emperor rules.

MAGPIE BRIDGE

Spanning the Milky Way, a flock of magpies formed a bridge with their wings. This Magpie Bridge reunited the lovers – the weaver girl and the cowherd.

MOUNT PENGLAI

This mountain lies on Penglai Island in the East Sea. The Eight Immortals are invited to a banquet on the island. In another myth, Boya learns to play the zither on Mount Penglai.

PRONUNCIATION GUIDE

Chinese is not a Romanized language and when translated into English, pronunciations and spellings do vary. There is also no clear emphasis of certain syllables. The names in this book are spelt out using the Pinyin system. This is a guide to how they sound in Mandarin Chinese, and are often pronounced in English.

Here's a general rule for pronouncing certain letters that you might find helpful:

"q" is similar to the "ch" sound in English

"x" is similar to the "sh" sound in English

"ü" is similar to the English "e-oo" sound

"e" is like the English "uh" sound

AO BING
ow bing

BA GUA
ba gwah

BEN CAO JING
buhn tsao jing

BO LE
boh luh

BOYA
boh-yah

BU ZHOU
boo joh

CAO GUOJIU
tsao gwoh-jyoh

CHANG'E
chahng-uh

CHENG LIAN
chuhng lee-an

CHEN TANG
chuhn tahng

CHONG YANG
chong yahng

CHU
choo

DAN ZHU
dahn joo

EMEI
uh-may

FA HAI
fah-hai

FAN XILIANG
fan shee-lyahng

FANG ZICHUN
fahng zee-choon

FENGHUANG
fuhng-hwahng

FU SANG
foo-sahng

FU XI
foo-shee

GONGGONG
gohng-gohng

GUANYIN
gwahn-yin

GÙN
goon

GUQIN
goo-chin

HANGZHOU
hahng-joh

HAN XIANGZI
hahn syahng-zee

HAN YI
hahn yee

HE XIAN'GU
huh syan-goo

HUAGUO
hwah-gwaw

HUAXU
hwah-shoo

JIANG TAIGONG
jyahng tai-gawng

JINSHAN
jin-shahn

JUN
joon

KUN
koon

KUNLUN
koon-loon

LAN CAIHE
lan tsai-huh

LAOZI
lao-zee

LEI FENG
lay-fung

LIANG SHANBO
lee-ahng shahn-boh

LI JING
lee jing

LONG PAO
long-pow

LÜ DONGBIN
lyu dong-bin

MA WENCAI
mah wuhn-tsai

MENG JIANG
meng jyahng

NE ZHA
nuh-jah

NIAN
nee-en

NIULANG
neeu-lahng

NÜWA
nyu wah

PANGU
pahn-goo

PENG
puhng

PENG LAI
puhng-lai

PENG MENG
puhng-meng

PUTI ZUSHI
poo-tee zoo-shr

QIAN LI MA
chee-en lee-mah

QIN
chin

QIN SHI HUANG
chin shee hwahng

QING MING
ching-ming

QIXI
chee-shee

QU YUAN
choo yoo-ahn

RUYI JINGU BANG
roo-yee jin-goo bahng

SHA WUJING
shah woo-jing

SHANG
shahng

SHANG JUN
shahng joon

SHANXI
shah-an-xee

SHAOXING
shao-shing

SHENNONG
shen-nong

SHUN
shoon

SUI REN SHI
swee-ren-shr

SUN WUKONG
soon woo-kong

TAIYI ZHENREN
tie-yee jen-ren

TANG SANZANG
tahng san-zahng

TANG YUAN
tahng-yoo-ahn

TIEGUAI LI
tee-eh-gwai lee

WEI
way

WEN
wuhn

XILING
shee-ling

XIN NIAN
shin nee-en

XI WANG MU
shee-wahng-moo

XU SHI LIN
shoo shee-lin

XU XIAN
shoo shee-en

YAO
yow

YI
yee

YU
yoo

YUAN XIAO
yoo-en shao

ZAO JUN
tsao joon

ZHANG GUO LAO
jahng gwaw lao

ZHANG YI
jahng yee

ZHE JIANG
jay-jyahng

ZHENJIANG
jen-jyahng

ZHINÜ
jee-nyu

ZHI YIN
jee-yin

ZHONG ZIQI
jong tsee-chee

ZHONGLI QUAN
jong-lee chwan

ZHOU
joh

ZHU BAJIE
joo bah-jee

ZHU YINGTAI
joo ying-tai

ZHURONG
joo-rong

GLOSSARY

ALCHEMIST type of scientist from long ago who tried to discover how to change ordinary metals into gold

ARRANGED MARRIAGE marriage planned and agreed by the families or guardians of the couple rather than by the couple themselves

BUDDHISM religion that follows the teachings of the Buddha, who lived in India about 2,500 years ago. Buddhists believe that the way to end suffering and achieve enlightenment, or nirvana, is though good behaviour and meditation

BUREAUCRACY administrative rules and procedures followed by organizations, such as a government

CALLIGRAPHY art of producing delicate handwriting using a brush or a special pen

CHAOS state of disorder and confusion

CHINESE BUDDHISM religion introduced to China by Buddhist monks from India in around 150 CE, which followed the same ideas as Buddhism, but with more of an emphasis on love of nature and with a less hierarchical structure

CICADA large insect, similar to a grasshopper or locust

CINNABAR red-coloured mineral found close to volcanoes or hot springs

CIVIL SERVICE government departments of a country, and the people who work in them

COCOON covering of silky threads that the larvae of moths and other insects make for themselves before they grow into adults

COMMEMORATE to remember an important event or person by a ceremony, action, or with a specially made object

CONFUCIANISM based on the teachings of Confucius, Confucianism is both a religion and philosophy that teaches the importance of good behaviour and family loyalty

COSMOS ordered and harmonious universe

CULTURE way of life and beliefs of the people of a region or country

DILEMMA difficult situation in which you need to decide between two or more alternatives

DYNASTY family of rulers whose power passes from one generation to the next

ELIXIR OF LIFE potion believed to extend a person's life forever, making that person immortal

EMPEROR ruler of an empire, such as Qin Shi Huang, who was the first emperor of China and ruled from 221–210 BCE as the first emperor of the Qin Dynasty

EMPIRE powerful group of states or countries governed by one ruling nation, such as the Chinese empire, which lasted from 221 BCE to 1912 CE

ENIGMATIC someone or something that is mysterious and difficult to understand

ENLIGHTENMENT state of reaching clarity of thought; in Buddhism, enlightenment is the final spiritual state in which everything is understood

FLINT type of sedimentary rock that splits into sharp splinters, called blades; flint produces sparks when struck

FORAGING collecting food in the wild

FRICTION force created when two surfaces rub or slide against each other

GINSENG root of a plant that is used in traditional medicine, especially in China

GUQIN ancient Chinese musical instrument with seven strings; the guqin is traditionally favoured by scholars

HAVOC great disorder and confusion

HEMP tough, fast-growing plant that originated in Asia and is used for making rope and for coarse clothing

HIERARCHY system of organizing people into different ranks or levels of importance, such as in society

IMMORTAL living forever

IMPERIAL things or people that are connected with an empire

INFERNO large fire that is out of control

LUNAR relating to the moon

MAGISTRATE type of judge in a law court who deals with minor crimes or disputes

MANTRA sound, word, or phrase that is believed to have spiritual energy and is used in meditation or prayer, especially by Buddhists and Hindus

MARTIAL ART form of self-defence and combat sport, often without weapons, that originated in East Asia, such as karate, judo, or kung fu

METAMORPHOSIS complete change of form or appearance, such as when a caterpillar turns into a butterfly, or a human becomes a god

METEORITE piece of rock or metal from space that has landed on planet earth

MILKY WAY strip of pale light made up of many stars that you can see stretched across the sky at night

MORAL relating to beliefs about what is right and wrong behaviour

MYTHOLOGY group of ancient stories from a culture that explains its legendary history, looks at the origins and nature of the world, and often features supernatural beings

NIRVANA state of enlightenment and peace; in Buddhism, nirvana is the highest spiritual state that can be achieved, in which everything is understood

PAGODA tall, highly decorated building, usually linked to Buddhism; pagodas are found in China, Japan, and throughout South East Asia

PERCUSSION group of instruments that produce rhythmic sounds when hit, such as drums or the triangle

PESTLE short, thick stick with a round end used for crushing things in a bowl called a mortar

PUPA insect with a protective covering that is in the stage of development between larva and adult

REINCARNATION belief that when a person dies, their spirit will be born again and live in the body of another person or animal

SAGE person who is very wise

SOLSTICE one of the two dates at which the sun reaches its maximum or minimum length – the summer solstice is the day with the most daylight hours, and the winter solstice has the least

SOULMATE someone with whom you share a close friendship and deep understanding

TAOISM both a religion and a philosophy, Taoism seeks a state of contentment and inner peace, free from desires and worldly influences

TRICKSTER mischievous character who likes to cause chaos and confusion

TRIGRAMS Taoist symbols of the cycle of Yin and Yang energy, which is present in all things

TYRANNY cruel and unfair ruler or government in which an individual or group have power over everyone else

VOID large, empty space

YIN AND YANG two complementary principles of Taoism: Yin is negative, dark, and female; Yang is positive, bright, and male. Together, Yin and Yang maintain the harmony of the universe and everything in it

ZEN BUDDHISM school of Buddhism; it originated in China

ZITHER class of musical instrument with strings stretched over a flat box; the guqin is a type of zither

INDEX

DK Penguin Random House

Written by Xiaobing Wang
Consultant Gang Liu
Illustrated by Katie Ponder

Senior Editor Marie Greenwood
Designer Bettina Myklebust Støvne

Managing Editor Jonathan Melmoth
Managing Art Editor Diane Peyton Jones
Senior Production Editor Nikoleta Parasaki
Production Controller Leanne Burke
Publishing Director Sarah Larter
Art Director Mabel Chan

First published in Great Britain in 2024 by
Dorling Kindersley Limited
DK, One Embassy Gardens, 8 Viaduct Gardens,
London, SW11 7BW

The authorised representative in the EEA is
Dorling Kindersley Verlag GmbH. Arnulfstr. 124,
80636 Munich, Germany

10 9 8 7 6 5 4
008–340069–Jul/2024

A CIP catalogue record for this book is available from the British Library.
ISBN: 978-0-2416-6476-6

Printed and bound in China

www.dk.com

MIX
Paper | Supporting responsible forestry
FSC www.fsc.org FSC™ C018179

This book was made with Forest Stewardship Council™ certified paper – one small step in DK's commitment to a sustainable future.
Learn more at
www.dk.com/uk/information/sustainability

The publisher would like to thank the following people for their assistance in the preparation of this book: Caroline Hunt for proofreading and Helen Peters for the index.

The author would like to thank: Marie Greenwood and Bettina Myklebust Støvne for their excellent editorial and design expertise, Katie Ponder for the beautiful illustrations, and my wife, Li Na, and daughters, Victoria, Olivia, Georgia, and Amelia, for their comments and suggestions on the stories.

ABOUT THE AUTHOR

Xiaobing Wang is an Economist at the University of Manchester, and the Research Director at the Manchester China Institute. He grew up in the suburb of Xi'an City in China. He loves reading and writing and has a deep understanding of the mythology of China. He lives in south Manchester with his family.

ABOUT THE ILLUSTRATOR

Katie Ponder is an award-winning illustrator whose work has been featured in exhibitions at Somerset House, and the DK books *Greek Myths*, *Norse Myths*, *Egyptian Myths and Goddesses & Heroines*. Her inspirations include ballet, ghost stories, and the greenhouses at Kew Gardens.

A NOTE FROM THE AUTHOR

The mythology of China draws its origins from a variety of sources, many of which date back to ancient classics such as *Shan Hai Jing* (or *The Classic of Mountains and Seas*), *Zhuangzi*, and *Records of the Grand Historian*. These stories have been further enriched and reimagined by later generations, becoming more complete. Some stories have their roots in traditional theatre, while others appear in literary works. Many tales were passed down through the oral tradition, and their authors are unknown. Some myths have been fixed for centuries, while others only began to take shape in the last century. In these retellings, I have used a little creative licence to help with smoother plot transition and logical consistency.